The Respected School Leader

This book offers an unprecedented look at a key component to becoming a collaborative, inclusive, and transformational school leader: respect. This practical resource takes you on a journey to achieve the highest level of respect as a school leader and includes a groundbreaking model that defines "respect" and provides you with specific tools to determine whether you've attained respect and how to leverage this for personal growth, success, and for sustainable school improvement. Case studies, stories, and narratives of highly respected school leaders are highlighted throughout. This book will provide you with all the self-reflection tools and exemplars necessary for your path forward to becoming a respected, inclusive, collaborative, and transformational school leader.

Howard J. Bultinck is a former superintendent and principal, and is Professor Emeritus/Department Chair of Literacy, Educational Leadership and Development at Northeastern Illinois University, USA.

Lynn H. Bush is a former assistant superintendent and principal and is Professor Emerita of Literacy, Educational Leadership and Development at Northeastern Illinois University, USA.

Noreen A. Powers is a former principal and current Associate Professor of Literacy, Educational Leadership and Development at Northeastern Illinois University, USA.

Also Available from Routledge
Eye On Education
(www.routledge.com/eyeoneducation)

Leadership Teams in America's Best Schools: Improving the Lives of All Students
Joseph F. Johnson, Jr., Cynthia L. Uline, Stanley J. Munro, Jr., Francisco Escobedo

Making Community Schools a Reality: Harnessing Your Power as a School Leader through Collaboration
Emily L. Woods

Wholehearted School Leadership: Rewiring our Schools for Courage, Justice, Learning and Connection
Kathryn Fishman-Weaver

Data Analysis for Continuous School Improvement, 5th Edition
Victoria L. Bernhardt

Culturally Conscious Decision-Making for School Leaders: A Toolkit for Creating a More Equitable School Culture
Shauna McGee

Teacher Leadership Practice in High-Performing Schools: A Blueprint for Excellence
Jeremy D. Visone

Coaching Education Leaders: A Culturally Responsive Approach to Transforming Schools and Systems
Nancy B. Gutierrez, Michelle Jarney, and Michael Kim

Fostering Parent Engagement for Equitable and Successful Schools: A Leader's Guide to Supporting Families and Students
Patrick Darfler-Sweeny

The Respected School Leader

Developing Your Character Traits and Transformational Leadership Skills

Howard J. Bultinck, Lynn H. Bush, and Noreen A. Powers

NEW YORK AND LONDON

Designed cover image: © Getty Images

First published 2026
by Routledge
605 Third Avenue, New York, NY 10158

and by Routledge
4 Park Square, Milton Park, Abingdon, Oxon, OX14 4RN

Routledge is an imprint of the Taylor & Francis Group, an informa business

© 2026 Howard J. Bultinck, Lynn H. Bush, and Noreen A. Powers

The right of Howard J. Bultinck, Lynn H. Bush, and Noreen A. Powers to be identified as authors of this work has been asserted in accordance with sections 77 and 78 of the Copyright, Designs and Patents Act 1988.

All rights reserved. No part of this book may be reprinted or reproduced or utilised in any form or by any electronic, mechanical, or other means, now known or hereafter invented, including photocopying and recording, or in any information storage or retrieval system, without permission in writing from the publishers.

Trademark notice: Product or corporate names may be trademarks or registered trademarks, and are used only for identification and explanation without intent to infringe.

ISBN: 978-1-032-26677-0 (hbk)
ISBN: 978-1-032-28298-5 (pbk)
ISBN: 978-1-003-29620-1 (ebk)

DOI: 10.4324/9781003296201

Typeset in Palatino
by Apex CoVantage, LLC

For my grandchildren: NJ, Emma, Grace, Caroline, Brooks, Ellery, and Collins

May you always remember your great-great-grandmother's words taped to a wall (modified from William Boetcker, religious leader and public speaker):

Your greatness is measured by your kindness;

Your education and intellect by your modesty;

Your real caliber is measured by the consideration, tolerance, and *respect* you have for others.

Grandpa Howard (Papi)

For my parents, Guy and Arline Franzese, who were my first teachers and leaders

For my children, Peter and Abby, and my grandchildren, Annabel, Lilly, and Lucas: May you be the first to offer respect and receive it in return.

Lynn

For my parents, Joe and Sal, brother, Dennis, and sister, Maureen, who are the guiding lights of my life.

My sincere appreciation is extended to my mother, who taught me respect.

My love and gratitude go to my children, Emily and Michael, my husband, and my sister, Colleen, who have encouraged and supported me throughout this process.

Noreen

Contents

Meet the Authors viii
Foreword. x
David R. Schuler
Preface xii
Acknowledgments xviii

1 **In Search of School Leader Respect: With All Due Respect**. 1

2 **Listening to the Voices That Determine School Leader Respect**. 17

3 **Mission, Vision, and Core Values** 40

4 **School Culture and Climate** 61

5 **Supporting a School's Well-Being**. 77

6 **School Leader Challenges**. 97

7 **School Leader Self-Respect** 116

8 **A School Leader: Respected and Transformational**. 133

9 **Measuring School Leader Respect** 152

10 **The Toolkit: A Step-by-Step Guide to Measuring School Leader Respect**. 165

Epilogue 176
Appendices 178

Meet the Authors

Howard J. Bultinck is Emeritus Professor in the Department of Literacy, Leadership, and Development, Northeastern Illinois University, Chicago, Illinois; an emeritus administrator search consultant with Hazard, Young, and Attea, Arlington Heights, Illinois; and a former teacher, principal, and 24-year veteran school superintendent at Sunset Ridge School District #29, Northfield, Illinois. He also served as Midwestern Advertising Manager for *Instructor* magazine. Howard J. Bultinck earned his Ph.D. from Northwestern University, Evanston, Illinois, in administration and policy studies and completed a post-master's program of study in curriculum and instruction at Northwestern. He earned his M.S. in educational administration from the National College of Education, Evanston, Illinois, and his B.S. in elementary education from Northern Illinois University, DeKalb, Illinois. He resides with his wife in Glenview, Illinois, and has three children and seven grandchildren.

Lynn H. Bush is Emerita Professor in the Department of Literacy, Leadership, and Development at Northeastern Illinois University, Chicago, Illinois. She is the coauthor, with Howard J. Bultinck, of the book *99 Ways to Lead & Succeed: Strategies and Stories for School Leaders* (2009). She is a former teacher, principal, and central office administrator. Lynn earned her Ph.D. in curriculum and instruction from the University of Illinois (Chicago); her M.Ed. in curriculum and instruction and educational administration from Loyola University, Chicago, Illinois; and her B.S. Ed. in elementary education and English from Drake University, Des Moines, Iowa. She resides in Western Springs, Illinois, with her husband, Jack, and has two children, two stepchildren, and nine grandchildren.

Noreen A. Powers is Associate Professor and Coordinator of the Educational Leadership Program in the Department of Literacy, Leadership and Development, Northeastern Illinois University, Chicago, Illinois. She is a former principal, assistant principal, curriculum director, and teacher. She has been in higher education for more than 30 years. Noreen earned her B.A. in psychology, her M.A. in elementary education, and her Ph.D. in curriculum and instruction from DePaul University, Chicago, Illinois. She resides in Western Springs, Illinois, with her husband, Jim, and has two children, Emily and Michael.

Foreword

Being a superintendent of schools or a building principal in Anytown, USA, is one of the most difficult jobs in the entire world, particularly in the past three to four years. It's one of the most important jobs in the world, but without a doubt one of the most rewarding. Make no mistake: America needs exceptional leaders for our school districts now more than ever. The challenges facing our students, our neighborhoods, and our democracy require leaders with an endless commitment and willingness to explore new solutions. Public education today is under a microscope. Forward-thinking district leaders are working diligently to create new sparks of joy and a fresh love of learning in their students in U.S. communities large and small. What's more, superintendents and principals are working to influence education policies that will have a lifelong impact on the young learners in their care.

After the COVID-19 pandemic, school system leaders now must choose how they're going to lead next. If we wish to leave no child marginalized and effect systemic educational reform, today's education leaders and their teams must give no less than 100 percent. All of us in education have the chance to inspire new dreams in the minds of our students as we continue to reshape and reimagine future-driven teaching and learning. In a post-COVID world, we need leaders to lead, not just manage.

I applaud Drs. Bultinck, Bush, and Powers for creating a blueprint for current and aspiring school leaders to help them gain new skills and reach greater heights in their careers. That's essential for our schools to thrive; our children depend on it. As administrators, we must foster a culture of respect among colleagues, staff, and the communities we serve. This respect is the bedrock underlying the educational experience and thus ensuring the success of our schools.

This book answers crucial questions for education leaders, principals, and superintendents, including: Are you a respected school leader? How do you know if you are respected? Why should you care about being respected as a school leader? – and all are invaluable insights for an impactful, productive, and accomplished career serving America's K-12 public school students.

David R. Schuler
Executive Director
AASA, The School Superintendents Association

Preface

"I respect our principal because when I meet with her, she gives me her undivided attention."

"He sure is a nice guy, but I don't respect him."

"She sure gets things done and treats people fairly."

"What a great boss; I truly love and respect our principal."

"It's great to see our principal engage with students at school events; I have a lot of respect for him."

"I don't know our new principal, but I'm looking forward to getting to know her."

Have you ever heard these comments made about the school leader where you work, or have you even said these statements yourself? The notion of school leader respect exists in a school, but the exact meaning is hard to pin down, and, as such, is even harder to attain. It is a non-discussable that educators nod that they understand, but somehow don't really know what it means.

The purpose of this book is to help you, the school leader, on your journey to being respected – it will show you how to validate with concrete measures your level of respect. We would ask you to consider four questions before you travel through this book and answer them honestly. You might even consider the questions like packing items in your suitcase for the trip. Are you ready? Here we go!

Are You a Respected School Leader?

Do school stakeholders (students, faculty, parents, and community members) come to a school environment where everyone who goes through the door is appreciated for the differences and values they bring? (Bultinck & Bush, 2009). Their contributions are important to the success of the school and, in turn, to the success of the school leader. You can learn your level of respect by implementing the ideas in this book. Additionally, you will be able to develop a professional development plan to increase the level of respect you have already attained.

How Do You Know If You Are Respected?

Are you guessing now? Are you saying to yourself, *Yes, people seem to like me. I assume they like me. My evaluations are very good and I still have a job, so I must be respected*. Besides skills, a school leader's personality must also be considered. There are humble leaders who may not even know they are respected because they are dedicated to being of service to their school and community and don't take the time to even think about it. On the other hand, some school leaders may be arrogant and believe they simply deserve to be respected – and often demand it.

Why Should You Care About Being Respected as a School Leader?

Because there is no doubt that the principal of a school is critical to school and student success. The work of Osborne-Lampkin et al. (2015) supports the concept that there is a relationship between the principal's characteristics and behaviors and student achievement in schools. Their compilation of studies yields strong evidence that this relationship exists. *The Respected School Leader: Developing Your Character and Transformational Leadership Skills* defines a school leader's level of respect by investigating the person's demonstrated skills and demonstrated attributes over time.

    The hope is that you can take a step back from the daily complexities and stress of school life and reflect on the values you are modeling. Are you doing your job well enough? Are you making an impact? By examining your own administrative skill set and personal attributes, you will become more effective in supporting others as a respected school leader and in all probability increase student achievement.

Another reason to care is because stakeholder relationships are critical to the success of the school. Those relationships are needed to move the school forward in a more efficient and effective way to see school impact.

How Can You Determine If You Are Respected?

The first step in discovering if you are respected is to allow yourself to become vulnerable. Brené Brown, in her book *Dare to Lead*, calls school leaders to action by asking them to be courageous, brave, and vulnerable. She states, "Leaders must either invest a reasonable amount of time attending to fears and feelings or squander an unreasonable amount of time trying to manage ineffective and unproductive behavior" (Brown, 2018). Checking in with your own behavior by looking at what stakeholders are saying about you through surveys and then plotting the results on the Respected School Leader Model will yield an honest picture of your administrative skills and personal attributes as they determine your level of respect as a school leader.

In this book, you will read about four respected school principals who have been determined to have achieved respect status by implementing the Respected School Leader Model using the research protocols discussed later in the book. These principals distributed surveys to all stakeholders and used the results to determine their level of respect. Three of the four principals were in the Chicago Public Schools (CPS) and the fourth principal was in a suburban Chicago school. Two of the CPS principals were in K–8 schools and one CPS principal was at a high school. The suburban principal was at a K–5 school. To ensure anonymity, pseudonyms were created for the principals: K–5 principal Elena, K–8 principals Luis and Vanessa, and high school principal John.

To assist you in your respect journey, you will find specific examples of how the daily work of our proven respected school leader exemplars has been greatly helped by being respected. To provide value-added, detailed stories and case studies are included, and reflection questions are posed. In addition, an appendix is included with data from the Respected School Leader Model research.

Are you willing to work on this? After all, willingness is essential when pursuing change. If so, here is a chapter-by-chapter preview of your respected school leader journey. Let's look!

In Chapter 1, "In Search of School Leader Respect: With All Due Respect," we provide background, discussion, and insight, and we define *respect* so that you can apply it in your leadership. The antithesis of *respect, disrespect*, is discussed as well, to help you navigate what respect is not. A visual structure (Maxwell, 2013) is provided to illustrate another way to see the steps toward respect and help to understand the task at hand. More challenges, background, and thought-provoking questions are offered so that you can be confident in the next steps.

Chapter 2, "Listening to the Voices That Determine School Leader Respect," introduces you to the students, faculty, parents, and community who have a vested interest in the school and school leader respect. Each group is discussed individually as to the need for respect in the school and from the school leader. Suggestions are given on how to facilitate each group regarding earning their respect.

Chapter 3, "Mission, Vision, and Core Values" discusses the critical importance of a school's mission, vision, and core values. Sample exemplary school mission, vision, and core value statements are shared as well as value-added commentary from four respected school leaders.

Chapter 4, "School Culture and Climate," focuses on a school leader creating a positive school culture that significantly contributes to a supportive school culture and climate. A positive school culture is essential for students to thrive academically, socially, and emotionally.

Chapter 5, "Supporting a School's Well-Being," draws attention to the importance of school leaders prioritizing the well-being of their schools. Respected school leaders realize that when they focus on the well-being of all stakeholders they are investing in the organic development and future successes of their entire school community.

Chapter 6, "School Leader Challenges," briefly but systematically lays out five of the greater challenges that school leaders face and reflects upon how they are called upon to deal with them. The respected school leader exemplars are highlighted and demonstrate how being this type of school leader is supported, encouraged, greatly assisted, and even a bit comforted when being respected.

Chapter 7, "School Leader Self-Respect," reflects upon school leaders needing to make time for themselves, away from their work of leading, to be more effective, productive, and successful. Unfortunately, it is hard to follow this advice in administrative practice. This chapter discusses and refreshes the reader about the concept and importance of self-respect and its links to being a respected school leader.

Chapter 8, "A School Leader: Respected and Transformational," discusses the transformational leadership approach and the behaviors necessary to achieve that style. Transformational leadership and respect are combined to challenge the school leader to see the benefits of a transformational approach and its relationship to earning and maintaining respect.

Chapter 9, "Measuring School Leader Respect," explains the Respected School Leader Model and provides the details and process to determine if a school leader is respected based upon the results of surveys from students, faculty, parents, and the school community regarding the school leader's skills and attributes.

Chapter 10, "The Toolkit: A Step-by-Step Guide to Measuring School Leader Respect," equips school leaders with comprehensive resources and guidance for effectively implementing the Respected School Leader Model. These essential tools and insights create a pathway for school leaders to be able to develop a collaborative professional development plan.

As Niyi Taiwo said, "If you desire respect, first explore your inner self to see if there is anything worthy of respect" (Taiwo, 2007). Our goal for this book is to inspire you with a practical resource for self-improvement and a guide to help you define and attain the highest level of respect as a school leader. We hope this book not only informs you and makes you stop and think, but also persuades you to be the best respected school leader.

References

Brown, B. (2018). *Dare to lead: Brave work, tough conversations, whole hearts*. Random House.

Bultinck, H., & Bush, L. (2009). *99 ways to lead and succeed: Stories and strategies for school leaders*. Eye on Education.

Maxwell, J. (2013). *How successful people lead*. Center Street Hachette Book Group.

Osborne-Lampkin, L., Folsom, J. S., & Herrington, C. D. (2015). *A systematic review of the relationships between principal characteristics and student achievement* (REL 2016-091). U.S. Department of Education, Institute of Education Sciences, National Center for Education Evaluation and Regional Assistance, Regional Educational Laboratory Southeast. Electronically published. http://ies.ed.gov/ncee/edlabs

Taiwo, N. (2007). *Respect: Gaining it and sustaining it: A comprehensive and practical view of the concept of respect* (Library of Congress Control Number 2007905971). Xlibris Corporation.

Acknowledgments

Writing a book of this magnitude is a team effort. To begin, we would like to express our gratitude to the following people who assisted us with our research: Marcie Byrd, Nestor Corona, Denise Dubravec, Otis L. Dunson, Christopher Gamble, Adam Greenberg, Mark Grishaber, Dr. Nichole Gross, Dr. Melissa Hirsch, Justin Johnson, Dr. Melissa Lewis, Heather Mathis, Dr. Josh McMahon, Israel Perez, Elena Ryan, Dr. Paul Sally, Brenda Stolle-Miramon, and Dr. Leticia Valadez.

We also thank our colleagues at Northeastern Illinois University: Kenny Beyer for his technical expertise, Jennifer Grzelak and Dr. Dave Kroeze for their support on our project, and Anderson Lam, IT Coordinator.

Special thanks to Susan Richter for her expertise in assisting us in editing our book.

Additionally, thanks to our publisher Heather D. Jarrow, who has made writing this book a pleasure from the beginning with her support and guidance.

Finally, thanks to our families for their patience and encouragement while we worked on this book.

1

In Search of School Leader Respect: With All Due Respect

It is difficult to think about respect without remembering the classic song from Aretha Franklin, "Queen of Soul," "Respect." Most people are unaware that Otis Redding wrote and recorded the song in 1965, but when Aretha Franklin released a modified version of the song in 1967, it became an instant hit, earning her two Grammy Awards in 1968. The timing of the release could not have been better, as the music resonated with women searching for equality, the Civil Rights movement, and the need for people to treat each other better with less discrimination and more respect. Aretha Franklin's words also encouraged the listener to find a personal meaning for respect and apply it in daily life (and, of course, spell it properly!).

Everyone wants to be respected. It is a natural and normal phenomenon that human beings want this personal characteristic for themselves. In Maslow's hierarchy of needs, the second tier of the pyramid is respect and self-esteem, while the highest is self-actualization (Maslow, 1943). It is easy to understand that Maslow's respect tier is extremely hard to attain, but he contends that individuals appear to be a work in progress and are motivated to grow to reach their potential as they move back and forth between the tiers of the pyramid (Maslow, 1987). Thank you, Maslow, but how do you define respect and how can a person reach that second tier on the pyramid as a school leader?

Trying to define respect in the world of school leadership is like beginning to learn a foreign language or observing and understanding an abstract painting on the wall. The word *respect*, just like the words in a foreign language or the strokes of a paintbrush in an abstract art painting, does not resemble anything one would know immediately until it is grounded. The word is abstract. *Abuela* in Spanish means grandmother, and when one sees the face of a grandmother or a house in the painting, it can be a revelation, even an "ah-ha" moment. Now I understand the words and pictures!

Besides being abstract, the concept of respect is ambiguous. This means that two people can define it differently and both be correct. One person could say, "I define respect in a leader as being trustworthy," and another person might say, "I define respect as how well a leader leads." Both are correct based on the individual's personal experiences, values, and beliefs. The word *respect* can even be grounded in how one was raised (Norville, 2009, p. 25; Taiwo, 2007, p. 127). It is the family value system that directs a child's behavior at an early age and encourages what is praised and what is discouraged. For example, one family may expect that adults who serve as authority figures, such as clergy and teachers, are treated with respect by younger members of the family. The family has assigned value and worth to those individuals. Another family may follow the "Golden Rule": "Do unto others as you would have them do unto you," meaning treat others as you would want to be treated. Each family may be different in its values, expectations, and responses regarding respect and how it is modeled in the home.

The definition of the word *respect* becomes clouded when other words are put in the definition such as *honest, attentive,* and *trustworthy*. For example, a teacher might say, "I respect the school leader because this person is honest, attentive, and trustworthy"; these are all abstract words based on an individual personal definition, which is unique in that it produces different perspectives and confusion. Tell me what you mean by *attentive*! What does it look like? Similarly, there is no doubt that the word *respect* can be slippery, complex, and very personal.

It may be time to consult the dictionary, past experts, and current authors who have offered definitions of the word to help formulate your own personal definition. The Merriam-Webster dictionary defines *respect* as a noun meaning "high or special regard: esteem." As a verb, *respect* means "to consider worthy of high regard." They appear to be similar, which can be of help when thinking about a definition.

The philosopher Immanuel Kant, in his early writings (Kant, 1785/1996), discussed who was worthy of respect and stated that "all persons are owed respect just because they are persons" (Dillon, 2022, p. 14). Kant's concept of respect serves as a human duty and one that should be protected and committed to in life. Respect for persons is essential because they are human beings. In her detailed article on respect, Dillon (2022) further discusses Kant's idea of a duty of respect as it appears in various contexts such as personal, social, political, and moral (p. 32). Dillion concludes by telling us there is still much work to be done in defining and implementing the concept of respect in our lives.

Some contemporary writers have written about respect as behavior and attitude, which may help in formulating a personal definition of respect. In school, respect as behavior and attitude can mean following the rules of listening and appreciating everyone's input on a problem so that everyone feels heard. No one is invisible (Westerberg, 2016). Examples of respect as behavior and attitude in everyday life could be following the speed limit when driving and allowing a faster driver to go in front of you or speeding to get an injured person to the emergency room. In some cultures, bowing can be a greeting of respect, an apology, or an expression of thankfulness, depending on the depth of the bow. And the list can go on. In summary, respect as behavior and attitude have elements of deliberation in that there is thinking and judging. In the school setting, the thinking may be, "What is it about this person, the school leader, that is worthy of my respect?" For example, the principal's behavior (an eye roll) was not appreciated at the meeting and was quickly perceived by others as demeaning toward a faculty member (judging).

Respectful leadership, as defined by (Ward, 2018), is the "Golden Rule," "Do unto others as you would have them do unto you." While we all know the rule and it is easy to say, it is not so easy to do because of the large assortment of behaviors and attitudes that we are willing to accept or not. Niels van Quaquebeke and Tillman Eckloff (2009) found this to be true in the workplace in general, and theirs appears to be the only in-depth research study on respectful leadership. This research study, *Defining Respectful Leadership: What It Is, How It Can Be Measured, and Another Glimpse at What It Is Related To*, examines what leadership traits are highly desired in a business organization not only by employees but by other stakeholders. They concluded that defining respectful leadership is problematic due to identifying concrete behaviors and traits desired by employees. Continuing their studies, van Quaquebeke and Eckloff investigated more areas such as followership, self-determination, and job satisfaction.

As school leaders, you may have come across the name John Maxwell. John Maxwell is a leadership expert. He is an author, speaker, coach, trainer, and pastor, just to name a few of his roles, whose work focuses on building strong leaders. One of his talents lies in being able to apply his thoughts about leadership to various workplace arenas, from large organizations, such as corporations, to small businesses and schools. But what is so appealing to school leaders is his practical perspective on how a person can grow slowly and steadily in their influence and followership as a leader by reaching various leadership levels with the people in the school community. His concept of "5 Levels of Leadership" (Maxwell, 2013) is a clear visual of a staircase filled with leadership expectations at each level. The design is a clear testament to the hard work it takes to climb to the pinnacle, which is RESPECT (Figure 1.1).

Maxwell's 5 Levels of Leadership

Maxwell's levels discuss the stages of leadership development and followership required by the leader as the person climbs the staircase steps toward the pinnacle, respect.

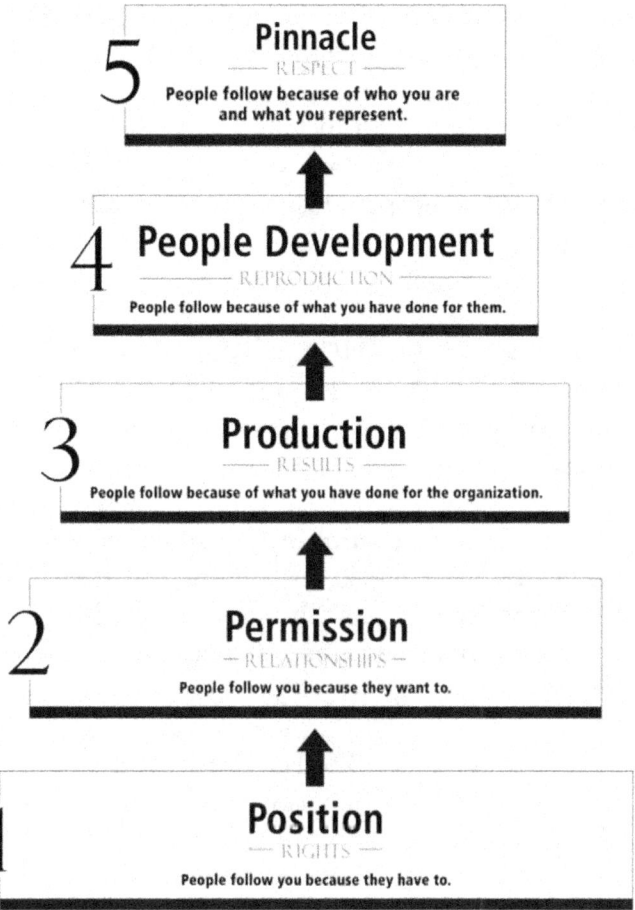

FIGURE 1.1 Maxwell's 5 Levels of Leadership: at the top, (5) Pinnacle/RESPECT; (4) People Development/REPRODUCTION; (3) Production/RESULTS; (2) Permission/RELATIONSHIPS; and (1) Position/RIGHTS

From *How Successful People Lead* by John C Maxwell, copyright © 2013. Reprinted by permission of Center Street, an imprint of Hachette Book Group, Inc.

The Levels of Leadership Explained

The principal will be used as the leadership example to make the levels more identifiable and applicable in the school setting. The faculty are used as the followers in the examples.

Level 1: Position/RIGHTS: This is the bottom level of the staircase. The principal was hired; therefore, the principal is respected by some because of the association of being in the position. The relationship that the principal has with a teacher, for example, is one of position: the boss.

> **What faculty might be thinking:** You have been hired in the position of principal, so I respect that. I have been taught by my family to respect people in positions of authority such as clergy, elders, police, and educators. (Lawrence-Lightfoot, 1999; Taiwo, 2007).

Level 2: Permission/RELATIONSHIPS: The school leader has taken the time and made the commitment to develop a working school relationship with the faculty in the school. (Barth, 1990; Brown, 2018)

> **What faculty might be thinking:** I like the positive working relationships we have in the school and how people get along. It makes me want to be an even better teacher so I do not disappoint my team of colleagues or my students. (Norville, 2009).

Level 3: Production/RESULTS: The principal reaches Level 3 of the staircase because the school community has been successful on other issues under that person's leadership.

> **What faculty might be thinking:** I like what we have accomplished as we progress to meeting our goals this school year. Our mission for success is alive and we have celebrated our successes as a school, so I will follow you as the leader.

Level 4: People Development/REPRODUCTION: This level is critical because the principal has made a commitment to help individuals grow and develop in their careers. This person has taken a genuine interest in faculty members in the school, brought out the best in others, and helped produce future school leaders.

> **What faculty might be thinking:** I like what you have done for me professionally as you support my growth as an educator. During my teaching evaluation meetings, you have offered opportunities for me to grow. Allowing me to serve

as the chairperson on important committees has helped my organizational and communication skills become stronger for myself and with my peers.

LEVEL 5: Pinnacle/RESPECT: This is the highest level, at which the principal is inspirational, influential, motivational, and creates a legacy of their work (Sinek, 2011).

> **What faculty might be thinking:** I follow you as a leader for the person you are and what you stand for. I am proud to be a member of this school because you are the leader. You inspire others and I want to be the best person and educator I can be under your leadership.

Maxwell's 5 levels of leadership raise many questions related to school leader respect. First, according to Maxwell, respect stands out at the highest step of school leadership at Stage 5 and similar to Maslow's Stage 4 (Maslow, 1943). Both Maxwell's staircase and Maslow's pyramid have ascending tiers. What specific traits are followers looking for? Do most school leaders attain this level? How will a school leader know when they have reached Level 5? Does it happen before or after you leave the school?

Within the 5 levels of leadership, it is possible that each faculty member may be thinking differently about their working relationship with the principal and may be at a different level with the school leader. For example, a first-year teacher might be on Level 1, as this teacher respects their new boss and is happy to have a job. However, a fourth-year teacher might be on Level 2 with the school principal because of the strong team relationships that have developed with this teacher and the opportunities to be a member of various curricular teams that have been given to the person. Multiply the number of teachers times all levels, and that yields the complexity of the school leader respect journey. In addition, Maxwell states the leader can go up and down the stair levels from time to time. This complexity of stair levels can be overwhelming to the point that a school leader may want to give up on the work of reaching the highest level. Maxwell allows the school leaders to figure it out for themselves, acknowledging that every school leader and school is different. Say no to giving up and yes to wanting to reach the highest level of school leadership: **Pinnacle/ RESPECT**. We're looking for a commitment here as a ticket to travel on the school leader respect journey. Are you ready? Oh, no, but wait!

People certainly can sense when respect is absent. Rodney Dangerfield, the comedian, made a living out of his classic routine, "I don't get no respect, no respect at all." In his routine, Dangerfield joked about his experiences when he was young, saying, "I played hide-and-seek; they wouldn't even look for me. In high school, when I played football, I got no respect – I shared a locker with a mop." While the words were said to an audience to make them laugh, they are real daily feelings to others of being rejected, neglected, ridiculed, taunted, and marginalized. It makes more sense to define the word in a positive way rather than a negative one, but, sad to say, some people are more familiar with disrespect than respect.

Our current and increasing societal actions of disrespect heavily influence the school environment and the personal experiences the school community has with respect. The school mirrors what is happening in society, and unfortunately, there is a new sense of urgency to discuss respect in schools due to the increase of disrespect as students bring their home and community life to school. Unfortunately, in some schools, the focus can be more on disrespectful behaviors for a school leader than strategies to develop a community of respectfulness. You might call it "putting out fires of disrespect" for the school leader, leaving little time to work on respect.

One Florida school district suggested banning school backpacks because they concealed what students were bringing in them (Rodriguez & Schwanemann, 2023). Therefore, it was suggested that students bring clear plastic backpacks with small personal items such as wallets, keys, and gym clothes to be kept in their locker. Everything was subject to search. This policy was intended to demonstrate safer procedures and a feeling of safety during the school day. Teachers were exempt from the policy, so some might see the policy as a double standard, one for students and one for teachers. Safety is certainly a priority in any school, but this policy might foster a feeling of mistrust and disrespect among students as well as a concern for how school leaders and teachers might implement the policy fairly. This proposed backpack policy was narrowly defeated, but it does bring up the question of how a school leader can ensure the safety of students and faculty while not sacrificing their personal respect.

"Putting out the fires of disrespect" is all too real in the practice of school leadership. Because the fires of disrespect need to be addressed, the school leader can be distracted. When some persons in schools are pushed to the edge, they may display extreme disrespect, and school leaders may witness disrespectful behaviors such as disruptive, demeaning, dismissive, nonverbal, and intimidating actions. To extinguish these immediate actions, school leaders can become distracted by putting more important tasks on hold, running out of time to complete required tasks, and losing focus and energy. Meanwhile, these fires become wild and all-consuming, possibly pushing a school leader to "burn out." Here are just a few fire examples:

- A **disruptive fire:** swearing at a teacher, telling school board members they are just like bobbleheads at a school board meeting, bullying, being inappropriately loud, accusing teachers of teaching a nonapproved curriculum, dealing with parents or community members insisting on books that should be banned from the library and ideas from classroom instruction.
- A **demeaning fire:** telling a child on social media that they are not valued, ridiculing a child's appearance, making threats with words, pictures, or cartoons.
- A **dismissive fire:** ignoring rules, challenging a teacher, interrupting a teacher during a lesson so that the teacher cannot finish the lesson, resisting doing work, not attending school, overlooking inappropriate behavior, cheating on tests, and talking over others.
- A **nonverbal fire**: making facial expressions of disgust, raising eyebrows, rolling eyes, pursing lips, and mouthing words.

An intimidating fire: stepping in front of others to get ahead in line, insensitive jokes, degrading comments about individuals in front of others, posting negative commentary about the principal online, threatening educators, and displaying a lack of civility.

Many of these fires of disrespect have been around in schools for decades, and it is not unusual for a school leader to "put out fires" as part of the job. Additionally, descriptions of the fires can overlap as some examples can be seen in several fire categories. They are not entirely new. What appears to be new is the intensity, volume, persistence, and catalyst for the fires. Why are some schools experiencing such intense and fiery disrespect?

One reason might be that our current societal environment is recovering from a lack of human interaction occurring during the COVID-19 lockdown and pandemic. The reliance on technology during the pandemic pushed individuals away from conventional ways of building relationships face to face, working and learning together, and problem solving. This lack of teacher-to-teacher, student-to-teacher, student-to-student, and teacher-to-parent interaction equaled social isolation because of the lack of opportunity for meaningful relationships. In some cases, individuals used texting, apps, chats, and other online platforms to display inappropriate aggressive behavior. The pandemic allowed some people to avoid being confronted for their behavior, become almost invisible, and hide behind technology.

While this behavior might have been overlooked just to get through the pandemic school years, technology encouraged some individuals to go down a very disrespectful road. For example, students who did not turn on their computer video screen during class could be doing other things such as texting, playing games, or bullying others. Not paying attention and not contributing to the discussion in a virtual class clearly shows disrespectful behavior toward the teacher and classmates. Technology distraction still exists, and many consider it disrespectful to attend to their personal devices, especially when there is an individual in front of them or when attending an in-person meeting.

Stress on school leaders, faculty, and students due to the pressure of delivering good test results can be an urgent catalyst for disrespectful behavior. School leaders might pursue a single-minded goal that overlooks the individual and the organization for the sake of their test scores. ACT/SAT and state and federal testing scores may become the focus of attention while teachers and students go unnoticed. Such behavior can cause competitiveness, academic dishonesty, inflexibility, and narrow-mindedness that reflect negatively on the school. As one mission statement on the wall in a high school said, "Our mission is to increase test scores." Yes, test scores, period. Anything else? This misguided statement can promote cheating and anxiety just to get an acceptable test score.

During the lockdown, parents became teachers and bedrooms and dining rooms were transformed into classrooms. Many parents had to become overseers of learning whether they wanted to or not. Some parents accepted this responsibility and others did not or could not. Some students quickly learned that they did not have to attend their virtual classes. Some attended haphazardly. This put parents in a difficult position. This behavior of negotiating with their students at home about the fundamentals of everyday classroom learning puts parents in the role of negotiators. Some students were debated what constituted being in class or the traditional routine of school and this carried over to the real classrooms when students returned to school. Today, some schools say attendance is suffering, and school leaders try to figure out how to get all students back in school. In the United States, 8 million students were chronically absent before the pandemic. A chronically absent student is defined as missing 10 percent of the school year. In 2022, that nonattendance rate doubled to 16 million, as reported by Mehta (2023) for National Public Radio and the research group Attendance Works.

Since the pandemic, some students have experienced anxiousness, fearfulness, and disrespectful behavior as they struggle to meet prepandemic academic standards. These learning gaps escalate disrespect toward teachers and peers, disguised as worry, concern, peer pressure, and panic over catching up on schoolwork. On March 3, 2023, one student high school newspaper described a higher level of student disrespect for teachers and classmates than before. Anger and outrage seem to be the first level of confrontation rather than irritation and conversation. (Tisopulos, 2023).

The push to flood political views upon schools is upsetting, unsettling, and disrespectful to the distinct uniqueness of every local school community. The blanket school experience for all is a myth, and school leadership and school learning are political. It always has been (Walker, 2018). Some politicians want to dictate what to teach (content), how to teach the content (instruction), and when to teach it (timing and age appropriateness). The new, questionable general laws stipulating a standard school curriculum and what can and cannot be taught, along with punitive polices for those who do not follow them cause great concern. These consequences can range from revoking teaching licenses and firing teachers to holding back state funding. This angers parents and school professionals. While this might seem oversimplified to say, school communities, namely local school boards, make decisions for the students, faculty, and staff in their charge, not politicians. Politicians telling educators what to do is like a patient telling a dentist which procedure to use when extracting a tooth or telling a plumber which tool to use when fixing a clog in a drain. Who has the expertise to be successful in a procedure or, in the case of a school, in devising strategies to attain successful learning using the curriculum for *all* students? The answer is the professional educator. And how is respect demonstrated and earned as the school leader navigates through the school's political arena? (Walker, 2018)

Some individuals think that school is primarily reading, writing, and math, and teachers and leaders should stick to that script. By imposing laws on what should be taught in academic areas and firing teachers and leaders for breaking the law, teaching and leading become something different than what educators signed up for. But schooling is so much more as school leaders concern themselves with the success of the whole individual in a respectful school community. As Deborah Norville (2009) says in her book *The Power of Respect,* maybe we should consider a fourth "R – reading, writing, 'rithmetic, and respect" (p. 93).

Why is there not more written about respect in professional literature for school leaders? Why is school leader respect a non-discussable in schools? The "non-discussable" is defined by Roland Barth (2002) as "the elephant in the room" – educators and parents do not want to address it but know it exists in the culture of the school. Respect clearly falls into the non-discussable category. Sometimes, a non-discussable can occur in a parking lot or in small group conversation among individuals in the school community. Conversation examples might be favoritism toward specific students, parents, or teachers. Another example might be a school employee who is not fulfilling their duties and it goes on unchecked. It might be a colleague who is not pulling their weight on a team. The conversation could even be about the school leader. These difficult conversations regarding respect are hard to facilitate by the school leader. Respect as a non-discussable causes fear in the individual who feels it is lacking, has an opinion, and is debating whether to bring it up. The conversation can be avoided if deemed too risky to mention to the whole group. It is better said in hidden arenas, such as parking lots or corners of hallways, where there are no consequences and the conversations can stay secret. The school leader may not have a clue there is a respect issue or may brush it to the side in favor of other pressing topics. Additionally, the school leader may assume or wish that the respect issue goes away and may choose to drop the idea prematurely. Whatever the thinking, the school leader must bring the respect issue to light with all its camouflage. If not addressed, it will grow like a rash into disrespect and dysfunction.

Individuals need more than a colorful respect poster taped in the hallway of the school or a banner decorating the classroom. It is the day-to-day environment of actualizing, enacting, and implementing the levels of respect that makes the difference. Respect must be lived every day in the school. If you stopped a person in the school hallway, could the individual explain what respect was in the school and what it meant to them? Does the school leader model respect in their everyday actions and interactions? Without deliberate intentions of demonstrating respect at school, can there be any real hope for the school leader to be respected? Because of the principal's status as the boss, individuals may feel uncomfortable talking about the lack of respect they feel for themselves and others and not address that with the school leader out of fear of jeopardizing personal and school health (Barth, 2002).

Everyone in the school sees the school leader through different lenses. For example, when individuals observe a video of the school leader speaking to a group, one person may focus on appearance, clothing, or stance, while someone else who observes the video may focus on the words that were said, not noticing the appearance, but observing the school leader in a different way. One person may think the speech was excellent, while the school leader might wish the presentation had been better. The point here is that perceptions and impressions have limitations, but to the person who sees and feels them, they are genuine, intrinsic, and real.

Others may come to define school leader respect by how they were raised, what they value, and their lived experiences. For example, some families do not make family time a priority, which implies that family members are not important. It is possible that there is no regular dinnertime with family, and instead five different meal preparations and each member of the family eating on their own schedule – thus missing the opportunity to listen to one another and interact.

A school leader is always on display, as the school community watches, judges, and forms opinions on appearance, facial expressions, interactions, and communication style. These impressions guide others to form opinions of the school leader that may be right or wrong but are opinions nonetheless and can be lasting. How do people in the school community see the school leader who is the prime respected role model for students?

The school leader in search of being respected should decide why this interest in being respected is important to pursue. Here are a few thoughts to help in the decision:

1. What is your personal definition of respect? Is the application of the definition the same in your school and school community? Is everyone pointed in the right respectful direction?

2. Where is the starting point for putting out the fires of disrespect as the leader begins to transform the school climate so that respect is the norm?
3. Why is it important for a school leader to think about this? Isn't a good school enough? If you've reached the crowning point in your career or are leaving a particular school district or position, here are some questions to consider: Did I matter at this school? Did I make a difference? What is the school leadership legacy I am leaving behind? Did I make this school a better place for students, teachers, and the school community than when I arrived? Was I respected?

A school leader can learn to be a respected school leader, and growth is the key. Expecting to be respected overnight is a fairy tale at best, but growth is the way toward professional improvement. Chapter 9, "Measuring School Leader Respect," is designed to help you acquire information and direction on the road to becoming a respected school leader.

In his book *Good to Great* (2001), Jim Collins poses two questions to the reader. First, "Why should I try to make it (the organization) great?" and second, "Isn't success enough?" Now apply these two questions to what school leadership might look like. As stated previously: "Why should I try to become a respected school leader? Isn't a successful school enough?" Collins states that if you are asking these questions, you might want to consider another line of work. Rather than answer these questions, you should ask not why but how a person should go about becoming a respected school leader and, in the process, making the organization great. (Collins, 2001, p. 209).

References

Barth, R. (1990). *Improving schools from within.* Jossey-Bass.
Barth, R. (2002). The culture builder. *Educational Leadership, 59*(8), 6–11.
Brown, B. (2018). *Dare to lead.* Random House.
Collins, J. (2001). *Good to great.* HarperCollins.
Dangerfield, R. (n.d.). https://www.imdb.com/name/nm0001098/quotes/

Dillon, R. S. (2022). Respect. In E. N. Zalta & U. Nodelman (Eds.), *Stanford encyclopedia of philosophy*. https://plato.stanford.edu/archives/fall2022/entries/respect/

Kant, I. (1996). *Groundwork of the metaphysics of morals* (M. Gregor, Ed. & Trans.). Cambridge University Press. (Original work published 1785)

Lawrence-Lightfoot, S. (1999). *Respect: An exploration*. Perseus Books.

Maslow, A. H. (1943). A theory of human motivation. *Psychological Review*, *50*(4), 70–96.

Maslow, A. H. (1987). *Motivation and personality* (3rd ed.). Pearson Education.

Maxwell, J. (2013). *5 levels of leadership*. Hachette.

Mehta, J. (2023, March 3). *3 years since the pandemic wrecked attendance, kids still aren't showing up for school* [Radio broadcast]. NPR. http://www.npr.org/2023/03/02/1160358099/school

Norville, D. (2009). *The power of respect*. Thomas Nelson.

Rodriguez, L., & Schwanemann, K. (2023, June 13). *Broward school board votes to scrap clear backpack policy*. https://www.nbcmiami.com/news/local/clear-backpack-rule-scrapped-broward-schools/3053131/

Sinek, S. (2011). *Start with why: How great leaders inspire everyone to action*. Penguin Group.

Taiwo, N. (2007). *Respect: gaining it and sustaining it. A comprehensive and practical view of the concept of respect*. Xlibris Corporation.

Tisopulos, M. (2023, March 3). End the uprise in disrespect to teachers from students. *The Wolfpacket*. https://www.thewolfpacket.org/9826/opinions/end-the-upside-in-disrespect-to-teachers-from-students/

van Quaquebeke, N., & Eckloff, T. (2009). Defining respectful leadership: What it is, how it can be measured, and another glimpse at what it is related to. *Journal of Business Ethics*, *91*, 343–358.

Walker, T. (2018, December 11). Education is political: Neutrality in the classroom shortchanges students. *NEA Today*. https://www.nea.org/nea-today/all-news-articles/education-political-neutrality-classroom-shortchanges-student

Ward, G. (2018). *The respectful leader*. Winding Creek Press.

Westerberg, T. (2016). The principal factor. *Educational Leadership*, *74*(1), 56–60.

2

Listening to the Voices That Determine School Leader Respect

Who are the stakeholders determining school leader respect? Are they the people in life who see the good first and share positive comments with the school leader? Are they the individuals who routinely step up to help and support the school? Or are they the squeaky wheels who call on the school leader regularly to seek time and attention, or the ones with friends in high places? They are the people, both internally and externally, in the school community who have formed personal opinions about the school leader.

While the topic of school stakeholders could be a book of its own, this chapter focuses on students and faculty, the internal school community, and the parents and community – the external school community. It addresses each deserving group of voices as a specific section so that their voices can be heard loud and clear. Two specific areas for discussion – stress and behavior – are chosen within each group to maintain focus and consistency. Suggestions for how a school leader might earn respect from each group while at the same time meeting group needs are also included.

Being uniquely different in their intentions and interpretations, school stakeholders, specifically students, faculty, parents, and other community members, have needs, goals, and perspectives, and it might even be said to be common ground. In no specific order, here are a few:

- The need to be a part of giving, receiving, and supporting a quality education. There is no debate about wanting a quality education for all students in school. Who would want a lesser or just adequate one? However, defining quality is another matter (think quality curriculum, quality program, quality teaching, quality teachers, quality school building, and on and on). After defining the word, there are the challenges of knowing when quality has been achieved.
- The need to belong – to be part of a group. Human beings need to belong and feel the relationship a group offers, such as friendship and connection (Karns, 2005; McLeod, 2024; Payne, 2003).
- The need to be treated in a caring, genuine, honest way (Brown, 2018).
- The need to be valued as a person, not belittled, dismissed, or demeaned. The key word here is valued, not patronized or talked down to. Most people can sense in a short amount of time when they are treated in a condescending manner, just as they know in a short amount of time when they are addressed and truly heard (Bultinck & Bush, 2009).
- The need to have a relationship with all stakeholders. For example, finding common ground and connections between the school leader, the school booster club, and the alumni association (Brown, 2018).
- The need to be heard on issues that involve them.
- The need to be informed about relevant information in a timely manner.
- The need to be engaged and ultimately feel ownership in the success of the decision-making of the school and receive recognition when goals are reached and celebrated (Lac et al., 2023; Shepherd & Williamson, 2022).
- The need to be part of a "good school." People want to say, "My school is a good school, and I am proud of it."

After all, no one ever wants to say, "I am part of a mediocre school."

Students

Louis Pasteur (n.d.) reminds us, "When I approach a child, he inspires in me two sentiments: tenderness for what he is and respect for what he may become." We all know that the reason schools exist is to educate students. Now say that another way, please: educating students is the reason for the existence of schools. Schools provide the space where teaching and learning can take place. Ask any school leader, when there are no students, faculty, staff, parents, or anyone else in a school building, what the school feels like. The reply might be, "It is an empty and cold place of bricks and mortar, lacking energy, joy, and the sounds of human interaction." Student voices are missed.

It can be frustrating and draining to students when their voices are not heard. They may feel others don't value them or don't care about them, or don't know what they need to learn at school. Possibly, this is why so many students act out, give up, or drop out. This isn't how students should feel in school! How often are students asked about what really matters to them about their learning? How often are they ever asked or heard?

But listening to student voices means more than just listening to students in class. It means listening to their collective voice and what really matters to them, such as in student government discussions in school. Granted, some younger students may not be able to articulate their needs, but primary teachers can speak up on their behalf if needed, and school leaders should listen to and respect the young voices as well.

Student Stress

Stress is real, unhealthy, detrimental, and sometimes fatal for students. For elementary, middle, and high school students, stress may look different than adult stress, but it is just as difficult and not any easier to handle. The postpandemic school years have been riddled with additional student stress, such as the stress to hurry up and learn to make up for the time missed! The usual school stressors exist, such as the need to work hard for good grades, undergo testing, deal with college admissions, overcommitment to outside activities, as well as family issues. Social media and bullying have produced harmful and suicidal effects. Add to the mix a lack of student confidence which might be demonstrated by anxiety, sadness, and fear. School leaders know that student mental health is a high priority, and 75 percent of high school students report feelings of anger, boredom, sadness, and fear as posted on Research.com on October 31, 2023 (Bouchrika, 2023).

Poor mental health and suicidal thoughts and behaviors increased from 2011 to 2021, as reported on the Centers for Disease Control and Prevention's (CDC) Youth Risk Behavior Survey (YRBS) of 17,508 questionnaires completed by 152 schools (CDC, 2023). In 2021, 10 percent of high school students attempted suicide one or more times during the previous school year. Female students were more likely than male students to attempt suicide, as were Black and LGBTQ+ students compared to their Caucasian and straight peers.

Improving student mental health means improving the school environment beyond a one-day emphasis like a Mental Health Awareness Day or assemblies. At school, a school leader can provide a consistent mental health climate based on what students must change in their behavior and what students need from the school to succeed. It might be a deep connection with the school leader, teachers, and peers. Creating that sense of belonging, feeling noticed, called by their name, and valued can make the difference between a student just existing at school and one who is thriving.

Student Behavior

Some students may be loud and offensive, exhibiting negative behaviors in school so they can be seen and be heard. Their voices are saying, "Notice me, so I am not invisible. Notice me, so I have your attention. I need it." These voices are time-intensive and require appropriate scrutiny by the school leader. Tim Westerfield (2016), retired principal of Littleton High School in Littleton, Colorado, writes that his first rule of respect is that no one is invisible. Genuine smiles, eye contact, and greetings were a part of his daily important contact with students to build continuing positive relationships so that connection can be used, especially during more trying times. This consistency can be viewed by students as a way to garner trust from the school leader and move toward earning student respect. The National Center for Educational Statistics (NCES, 2022) states that some recent poor school behavior can be attributed to the loss of school routine and proper behavior development following the pandemic. More than 80 percent of public schools surveyed reported that the pandemic negatively affected student behavior and socioemotional development during the 2021–22 school year. Four student behaviors were mentioned in the report and appear to have had a lingering effect:

- Classroom disruptions from student misconduct (reported by 56 percent of schools).
- Acts of disrespect towards teachers and staff (48 percent of schools).
- Rowdiness outside the classroom (49 percent of schools).
- Use of prohibited electronic devices (42 percent of schools).

Clearly, stress and poor student behavior are two actions among others that diminish school respect and reignite the embers of disrespect. Turning disrespectful student behavior into respectful behavior starts with the school leader putting student relationships first. How school leaders respect student voices by prioritizing their concerns can make the difference between a successful student and one who is disengaged from school.

What should the school leader keep in mind when thinking about student voices and earning their respect? What might students sound like? Who am I? What am I expected to do in this school? How do I fit in? Should I join this activity? Am I safe here? Who is the school leader? How do I make new friends? Who are my friends? Am I respectful, kind, and caring, a class leader, a good test taker, a fast learner, a homework doer, a rule follower, an influencer, an athlete, a student in the background, a teacher pleaser, a class clown, an excuse maker? And so on.

How can school leader respect help students? The following list has some ideas.

- Setting school boundaries in academics and behavior can defuse aggressive student "noise." For example, when a student wants to argue, try to set the tone and even take over the conversation and create a student plan. This boundary tells the student the game is up and the focus has changed. One strategy is for the school leader to explain a plan containing respectful, positive behaviors involving student respect and using statements such as, "I listen, but I don't argue." This authoritarian approach works at the beginning when dealing with school behavior problems because it can soften into an agreeable, respectful plan with student support, follow-up, and a timeline, thereby reducing the struggle for everyone involved.
- Knowing students' names, families, and individual student interests and "showing up" for them (Brown, 2018, p. 9) displays respect and gives students a feeling of being valued. And yes, this can be done even in a large school.
- Being visible at school events builds on all stakeholder relationships and connections.
- Offering more before- and after-school activities, clubs, and athletics to offset stress, such as peer-to-peer and teacher-to-student tutoring, can help students get into the rigorous school routine. Other activities, such as video gaming, knitting, crocheting, or yoga, help facilitate belonging. What the school can offer depends on the age of the students in the school as well as the parents' needs and finances for after-school care.

- Currently, one suburban Chicago public high school offers 130 activities and athletics to provide opportunities for students to become engaged in the total school community and learn leadership skills and responsibilities as a change of pace from academics. Eighty-five percent of the student population has chosen to participate in activities and athletics. There is even an opportunity to start a new club if a student is interested and the requirements and contacts are listed on the school website (www.lths.net/activities).
- Giving students opportunities to demonstrate respect provides the school leader a measure of how respect building is working. For example, learning to listen to those who have different opinions and values even though they may disagree and recognizing that the person is entitled to their opinion is a good sign that respect may be working among students. School leaders modeling respect in the hallways with all stakeholders is a must.
- Communicating quickly when changes in schedules, events, and situations occur.
- Keeping school spirit alive and highlighting the positives every day.

Student stress and discipline are not new to the work of school leaders. What is new is the attention, priority, and dedication that student voices require during this challenging time in education.

Let's give students the attention they deserve and assume they are doing the right thing at school until the school leader learns otherwise (Westerfield, 2016). Let's listen to what they are saying (or not saying) and make ongoing relationships with students a priority. We should be centering them with the attention of the school leader (Lac et al., 2023), praising them for their efforts and successes, honoring their participation toward meeting school goals, and listening, asking, and respecting them for the wonderful people they are. This can advance the school leader's progress toward earning student respect.

Faculty

Who are the faculty? The term *faculty* refers to a body of educators (i.e., teachers or professors) whose aim is to impart knowledge to learners at schools, colleges, and universities. The faculty is hired for the purpose of providing education to their students (Surbhi, 2023).

By comparison, the word *staff* has a broader meaning and includes all employees working in the school organization (Surbhi, 2023). This includes faculty, counselors, speech/language pathologists, nurses, social workers, teacher aides, teacher assistants, secretaries, security guards, lunchroom supervisors, bus drivers, custodians, and so forth. Additionally, administrators such as deans, directors, assistant principals, coordinators, and department chairs are considered administrative staff.

For clarity, in this book and survey examples in the toolkit, the term *faculty* is used as defined previously and not staff. The words *faculty* and *teacher* are used interchangeably and synonymously.

Faculty Stress

Breaking news!! Faculty stress is alive in schools. Stress has always been seen as a workplace hazard in education, but during and after the pandemic, faculty stress has been highlighted, aggravated, and elevated. A Rand Corporation survey of more than 1,000 teachers in 2020–21 found three areas that produced great stress for teachers. The first area was the mode of instruction, namely hybrid teaching (in-person teaching and remote instruction combined). The second was concerns about the faculty's health and the health of their families, and finally, the third stress area was insufficient pay, given the risks and concerns in daily teaching and learning. Additional findings reported that these stressors contributed to the possibility that faculty would not stay on the job (Steiner & Woo, 2021).

So are teachers okay? At a speech to the National Education Association (NEA) annual delegate assembly on July 4, 2023, U.S. Secretary of Education Miguel Cardona told the educators, "You went from pandemic to persecution, and in some parts of the country, they've developed an intentional, toxic disrespect for public school teachers." As a solution, Cardona proposed what he called the "ABCs of teaching," which stands for agency, better working conditions, and competitive wages. (Will, 2023a). This government support is gladly welcomed.

But are teachers okay? Feeling better? There seem to be some indications that teachers are happier than in past years. Teachers state that teaching has gotten a bit easier than the reentry year from the pandemic due to fewer disruptions to the school calendar, classroom schedules, and teacher expectations, all of which help students adapt to school routines (Will, 2023b).

Faculty Behavior

The pandemic and the subsequent Great Resignation – in which many workers simply left their jobs – gave many Americans time to reflect on their career pathways and consider changes. The healthcare, retail, service, and technology industries were hit the hardest, and workers gave these three reasons for leaving their positions: low pay, no opportunity for advancement, and lack of respect at work (Parker & Horowitz, 2022). The feeling of lack of respect in the teaching profession seems to have followed this trend as well.

People come to the teaching profession to make a difference in the lives of students. When that longing is shattered, teachers begin to reflect on making changes. The postpandemic residue left over from hybrid teaching and the frustrations and concerns over the lack of student academic progress are two of the reasons that have led many teachers to abandon their profession and search for new career options.

What jobs have teachers found? Many of the skills that teachers have are desirable in the business world such as at technology companies, business training departments, and educational publishing firms. Many teachers have the instructional design skills to create digital courses, training sessions, materials, and manuals. Teachers can take complex ideas and break them down into manageable lessons, formulate timelines for completion, and assess results. Teachers can establish goals, follow guidelines, and construct plans, while understanding what adult learners need on a day-to-day basis. Teachers know what teachers need in other education businesses and can provide specific skills in the form of writing grants, articles, or professional development tools and essentially become independent contractors and freelancers determining their own schedules and pay (Gomez, 2022). And this is just the beginning of possibilities.

This faculty behavior of leaving the profession has created a domino effect, with teachers leaving their positions and few qualified applicants available to replace them. Some years ago, there was a lack of speech therapists, math teachers, and bilingual faculty. Those positions are still unfilled in many school districts, given a weakened educational system looking for specialized, certified faculty. Add a pandemic, and presto! – the result is a severe teacher shortage.

Data sources taken from Research.com, NEA, *Education Week*, Educators for Excellence, Adopt a Classroom, and MDR (a division of Dun and Bradstreet) were compiled for an easy-to-read report with 18 teacher-shortage statistics findings and one bright light. These interesting 2023 teacher shortage statistics appeared on the We Are Teachers website (Staake, 2024). They are alarming but certainly not unexpected. The glimmer of hope from this research is that 66 percent of teachers are "satisfied" with their job. Teachers still have passion for their work. This is an increase from 2022, as found in the *Education Week*/Merrimack poll. It was reported that job satisfaction was up from 56 percent (Staake, 2024).

Linda Darling-Hammond, Professor Emeritus at Stanford University and expert in the field of school policy, equity, and quality of teacher education and teaching, saw the current teacher shortage coming. She even experienced a teacher shortage personally. In 1970 she agreed to become a teacher due to a teacher shortage with the added benefit of government loan forgiveness contained in the National Defense Education Act. This helped reduce the shortage, but only temporarily. The cycles of teacher shortages appeared again in the 1980s and early 2000s. The author of more than 25 books and more than 300 articles, Dr. Darling-Hammond has been a consistent champion for teachers' voices by rethinking how teaching is seen as a profession. Just as some teachers used the pandemic to reimagine their career pathways, Dr. Darling-Hammond suggests the time is now to help transform the pathway and the profession of teaching. Her suggestions involve taking lessons from countries such as Finland, Canada, and Singapore. However, these ideas will not go far without the support of the federal government. Therefore, she suggests a plan that would include six actions: 1) strengthen recruitment with government incentives; 2) improve teacher preparation; 3) support beginning teachers through high-quality mentoring programs; 4) offer job-embedded professional development; 5) establish grants for those schools that wish to re-create schools involving students, educators, and families; and 6) reauthorize the Elementary and Secondary Education Act to measure actual factors toward school improvement and remove unnecessary testing actions that yield inaccurate data (Darling-Hammond, 2022).

Suggestions and ideas for teacher retention and solving the teacher shortage are widespread in educational literature, with some examples presented previously. One shining light working on improving teachers' salaries nationally is called the Teacher Salary Project. The aims and goals of this nonpartisan organization are to influence federal legislation to stop underpaying and undervaluing teachers.

What should the school leader keep in mind when thinking about teacher voices and earning respect? What might faculty voices sound like? I don't have time for this. I am exhausted. I enjoy working with my colleagues at this school. That policy doesn't make sense for kids. When are they going to get a permanent teacher for that room? Will the school leader support me on this difficult call to a parent? I don't feel safe, too many unknown people are roaming in the hallway. Do I have the resources I need for my students? Does the school leader know what is going on in my classroom? I don't feel that some parents respect me as a professional. I spent two days preparing for that workshop for my colleagues and it went well. Some of my students are still struggling academically from the pandemic. I need help for them. The importance of addressing concerns brought to the school leader or communicated indirectly cannot be underestimated. If these voices are ignored or dismissed, the principal–teacher relationship can crumble and produce a loss of respect.

How can school leader respect help faculty? To say the least, earning faculty respect is a challenge for any school leader. It's like looking at a high jump bar at a track meet and wondering if you can make it over. School leaders need to find ways to reduce teacher stress and find out how teachers are feeling to gain their respect. Are teachers really okay? In their hearts and minds school leaders most likely know and should care. The workload in any organization is demanding and intense, but in the school organization, if the school leader knows the pulse of the school, then the leader knows when excessive demands on time and energy are taking their toll on the faculty. Here are some ways the school leader can help reduce teacher stress and continue traveling the road to earning faculty respect.

- Model respect for teachers.
- Look critically at what the school organization or district is asking teachers to do. Is teacher energy and time being spent productively and efficiently?
- Place a high priority on people and relationships (Tomlinson, 2018).
- Create teacher teams for various reasons, such as implementing ideas, addressing problems, and designing guidelines for transforming learning. Make sure to schedule meetings for the teams. Teachers can feel the strength of belonging to these teams (Brown, 2018; Hoerr, 2009).
- Finish and apply the work that teachers do and are proud of, thus allowing them to feel valued, appreciated, and recognized (Dill, 2022).
- Stand up for and protect teachers' time when policies are top-down and do not include any teacher voice.

- ♦ Check in with the faculty personally and professionally and monitor their health (Will, 2023b).
- ♦ Support and act on teacher concerns for students' academic, mental, physical, and social wellness (Will, 2023b).
- ♦ Trust teachers in their knowledge and craft of creating meaningful learning.

Let's give teachers the attention they deserve. Faculty want voice and choice in practicing their profession. The current literature and research support teacher needs and concerns and suggest what school leaders and policymakers could do to reduce and support teachers. Faculty want a voice and choice in the pedagogies of teaching, specifically the content of their classes as well as the autonomy on how to teach it. (Darling-Hammond, 2022; Will, 2023b). They want a voice in the decision-making process that affects them and their students in school, such as class scheduling, instructional planning, and policies pertaining to discipline (Dill, 2022; Will, 2023b). Additionally, postpandemic student behavior is a concern for faculty because when there are constant discipline disruptions in the classroom, classroom instruction is interrupted, frequently stopped, or, in some cases, dropped for the day, greatly affecting student learning in the classroom.

Faculty want to be recognized as the superstar professionals they are and properly paid in line with other professions that have similar credentials. When faculty are pushed over the edge, they will want to leave the classroom. It doesn't make sense to lose valuable professional educators when school leaders have spent so much time and money hiring, guiding, coaching, and supporting them in their work. Respect costs nothing and adds tremendous daily currency.

Parents/Parent Stress

Parenting during the school years is a difficult, stressful, and expected responsibility. Just like students and teachers, parents are looking for what might be called a "normal" postpandemic school year. Setting school routines at home, such as when and where to do homework and bedtimes, and juggling before- and after-school activities, can be a challenge since it is different than when students were learning at home. Parents expect schools to keep their children safe, prepare them for the future, and support them in their learning. Or have situations changed?

Surprisingly, for some parents, the pandemic seems to have changed educational goals for their children significantly. In a national poll of 1,010 adults conducted by YouGov in September 2022 and a Populace Insights study told to Axios by Todd Rose, Collins (2023) reports on a disparity in what society wanted for students in the past and what parents in K–12 schools expect for their students in the future. Parents' top goal for K–12 isn't a path to college or high wages. The survey found it appears that parents are more interested in seeing their children follow their own interests and be prepared for basic life skills like taking care of themselves and managing finances (Collins, 2023).

A YouGov poll of 57 educational priorities for adults rated "college preparation should be the ultimate goal for K–12 education" 47 out of 57. Three additional student priorities rated higher than the goal to attend college (Collins, 2023) were:

- Develop student character, such as problem-solving and decision-making
- Receive the basic skills of reading, writing, and arithmetic
- Support student needs throughout their learning

Other priorities listed in the poll but not given a rating number like the educational priorities listed previously were:

- Education should be individualized, rather than "one size fits all." Assessing students based on standardized testing was given low priority while allowing students to pursue their interests was rated high.
- Race makes a difference in ranking education goals with some overlap. Racial groups shared an interest in developing critical thinking and practical skills, but some school priorities were very different. For instance,

"being prepared to be a productive member of society is the fifth-highest priority for Hispanics compared to White (No. 48), Black (No. 39), and Asian (No. 30) respondents."
- ◆ The goal of education should not be "better" but "different."

Clearly, these studies might suggest a trend and deserve school leaders' attention, as some parents point toward a new direction away from traditional priorities for their children. Parents are looking for other options and expect schools to support their children individually in those choices.

Parent Behavior

Parents are a child's first teachers and model the attitude and the expectations the family has about school and education. For example, when a parent specifically blames the school or teacher when their child doesn't do schoolwork or do well on a test, the message to the student is clear: "I don't have to do my work because my parent will tell the teacher I don't have to do it." Regrettably, even being disrespectful to a teacher in front of a child or while on the phone can foster a poor attitude leading to disrespect.

Usually, students want their parents and teachers to like each other, get along, and want the best for them as they progress through school. Students want to feel supported. When parents blame teachers for a child's poor grades, behavior, or attitude, or the reverse, when the teacher blames the parents for their child's poor grades, behavior, or attitude, little is accomplished and the kindling of a fire of disrespect can start.

Staying positive about school, even when a child is having difficulty, can be challenging. One option that has opened since the pandemic is the number of online opportunities for students and parents to seek help or foster student interest (Collins, 2023). A plethora of online tutoring options is available. Let's say a child might have an interest in a foreign language; if it is not offered at their school, students could begin lessons on their own time schedule at home. Parents have many more options if they stay positive.

Another example of positive school parenting was at the beginning of the 2023 school year in one school attendance area. Parents wrote in chalk on each cement sidewalk block kind and encouraging back-to-school messages. Some were outside of their homes, and some were on the way to school. Each sidewalk block was colorful. Some of them said, "You can do it!" "Make a new friend." "I am so very proud of you." "You will make a difference." "Have the best school year."

What should the school leader keep in mind when thinking about parent voices and earning respect? What might parent voices sound like? Is my child safe when they are at school? How can I support my child's teacher and school? Is my child getting a quality education? Should I join the parent-teacher organization? Are students and adults treated in a caring way? Is the work that parents do for the school appreciated? Are parents viewed as more than fundraisers? Do I have a voice in my child's education? Is my child attending a good school? If I have a school question, who do I call directly?

How can school leader respect help parents? Some ideas include:

- Be visible and available to answer questions, guide, and support parents.
- Make sure parents feel welcomed and comfortable in a positive school environment.
- Look for avenues for parents to become active partners in the classroom and in the school and notice if parents feel the partnership.
- Know family and student names.
- Review and remind parents of the information channels they may need.
- Follow through with promises, emails, and phone calls.
- Emphasize positive school parenting.

Providing space and time to meet and then stepping back to listen is a way to build respect among school leaders. However, there is a fine line for the school leader to traverse: be careful not to step back too far, as this can be misunderstood by parents, giving the impression of stepping away or not being interested. Rather than checking in and showing up, school leaders need to stay attentive and follow up.

Let's give parents the attention they deserve when they say they want the best for their children in school. Building respect and closing the distance gap between families and schools takes hard work and many opportunities for interaction and conversation about concerns with the school leader. Giving all parents and families a feeling of being welcomed at school is important, especially for families of marginalized students (Lac et al., 2023). Building on the traditional role of parent involvement in school as fundraisers and service providers toward an additional role of parents as genuine partners with ideas and opinions to share can yield a new dimension to school problem solving, decision making, and guidance for the school leader. "Rather than asking what parents can do for the school, ask what schools can do for parents" (Lac et al., 2023). Additional events, both formal and informal, need to be available beyond parent-teacher conferences, open houses, curriculum nights, parent universities, and impromptu hallway conversations. New groups can be formed, such as parent advisory action groups that meet regularly or on demand on topics such as bullying, internet safety, and respect. This extra effort by the school leader can establish trust on one hand and build powerful parent relationships of respect on the other.

Community/Community Stress

It doesn't take much for members of the community to react to rumor and hearsay. Sometimes, local newspapers create concern through the headlines they use and the stories they print, such as "School administrator salaries in Town X highest in the state" or "State test scores at XYZ School still below state average level."

Some community voices may react to rumor and hearsay like bugs trying to escape insecticide: scrambling, buzzing, and flying here and there. Or it could be an online blog or a community influencer who likes to write daily or something as simple as two people who meet at the local grocery store and share stories. Pointing fingers about who is right and who is wrong and what is happening in the community wastes considerable time and energy from community members as the school leader takes on the role of referee.

A school leader needs to reflect on these questions: Who are your key communicators in the community? Who are those in the know and who are strong influencers of others? Check out the online news sites, blogs, and other websites for those who comment regularly about school. What is going on at the Rotary Club, local library, government officials, women's clubs, realtors, small businesses, chain businesses such as Starbucks, Walmart, Target, and Kroger, local fire and police departments, and among those citizens who do not have children in school? Additionally, the positive school community leaders who serve on school boards or are school trustees need to be respected, thanked, and appreciated.

Community Behavior

Many local school communities are under stress as they work through world, national, and local politics, which creates social and emotional issues for individuals who reside in the community. One example that creates pressure for communities to address is book bans. Small groups of people appear to be protesting to local school boards about which books should be removed from the school libraries and what should be removed from the curriculum. This behavior causes emotion, concern, and tension for members of the community to take sides or rethink what is best for students in school. These community actions can have harmful effects on students as they watch stories of books being removed from classrooms and library shelves, especially for students in marginalized communities. Additionally, faculty and staff may be disciplined or threatened with dismissal for going against community opinions and, in some cases, state laws. This community behavior causes the relationships between parents, faculty, students, and the school leader to deteriorate. This is one example that could easily transfer to a similar scenario for other community issues, such as selling school land and school buildings, changing student school boundaries, grading or not grading homework, raising taxes, and so on. It turns school leader respect on its head, dominates discussions, and is an unfortunate setback for developing school leader respect.

What should the school leader keep in mind when thinking about community voices and earning respect? What might community voices sound like? How do the school's reputation and students reflect on my business or organization? Are students receiving a quality education? Are we legitimate partners in education or are we partners on paper only? Are there groups at school for adults in the community that would welcome me as a member? Am I treated in a welcoming way when I contact the school? Do I receive recognition from the school when I support various requests? Is the communication frequent beyond the school board/trustee minutes and newsletters? Do I have a relationship with the school leader? Has the relationship with the school been a long-term one? Why are our taxes going up?

How can school leaders respect help? Some ideas include: Building relationships through opportunities to get together when things are calm in the community lays the foundation for trust in times of crisis and uncertainty. Having meaningful events where students, faculty, parents, and community members can interact and share insights helps to dispel rumors and develops relationships supporting school leader respect. One idea might be to have an essential theme for the school year, such as community volunteer opportunities for students or school mental health and well-being. Community organizations can take the lead in activities such as Breast Cancer Awareness Month, talent shows, and trivia competitions, to name a few ideas. Bringing older students back as peer mentors or "buddies" or teaming up with organizations that share an interest in community gardens are other possibilities.

One may not know when community support will be needed. Enlisting community members' help in time of need can frequently be counted on, provided the foundation of community-based relationships is strong. The key is communication. If the school has a public relations director or community relations coordinator, it shows the school has a high regard for working with its community. However, without staff in that position, the school leader must spearhead these efforts.

Let's give the school community and all its members the attention they deserve. Most bankers, businesses, and government officials usually do not approach schools first. The school leader needs to take the first step by opening the school door. That first step could be getting an important school message out before others do or asking key communicators the best way to send the message if time permits. Giving space, time, and attention to those voices in the community so that experiences at school are positive and welcoming is another step. Additionally and concurrently, the school leader is learning from the wisdom of the group. These steps can go far in taking a reading on the school leader's respect thermometer – or as Manuel Corazarri (2024) states, "The easiest way to open a closed door is with kindness and respect."

Schools are accountable to the communities they serve and should not isolate themselves from their local communities. They offer opportunities for schools and community members to become genuine partners in working toward student success. The pandemic taught schools how difficult it was to operate in the absence of a community and how dependent each is on the other.

To summarize this chapter, each stakeholder group – students, faculty, parents, and the community – seeks respect from the school leader and can grant individual and collective respect. No one specific group voice should be overlooked, ignored, or put above the other. To do so could produce negative respect consequences such as increased tension and resistance to support to meet student goals and school initiatives from a group. Failing to listen honestly and ethically can also create a school environment where group perspectives are overlooked, falsely assumed, and not respected. On the other hand, the hard work that it takes to honor and listen to these voices pays high-yield respect dividends.

References

Bouchrika, I. (2023, October 4). *50 current student stress statistics: 2023 data, analysis, and predictions*. Research.com. https://research.com/education/student-stress-statistics

Brown, B. (2018). *Dare to lead*. Random House.

Bultinck, H., & Bush, L. (2009). *99 ways to lead and succeed: Stories and strategies for successful school leaders*. Eye on Education.

Centers for Disease Control and Prevention. (2023). *Youth risk behavior survey: Data summary and trends report*. https://www.cdc.gov/healthyyouth/data/yrbs/pdf/YRBS_Data-Summary-Trends_Report2023_508.pdf

Collins, L. M. (2023, January 19). Parents' top goal for K–12 isn't path to college, high wages: Survey. *Deseret News*. https://www.deseret.com/2023/1/19/23560986/parents-top-priority-for-education

Corazarri, M. (2024, October 16). *Quotes about respect in relationships*. Mom Junction. https://www.momjunction.com/articles/quotes-about-respect-in-relationship_00782208/#150-respect-in-relationship-quotes

Darling-Hammond, L. (2022). Breaking the legacy of teacher shortage. *Educational Leadership, 80*(2), 14–20.

Dill, K. (2022, June 20). School's out for summer and many teachers are calling it quits. *Wall Street Journal*. https://www.wsj.com/articles/schools-out-for-summer-and-many-teachers-are-calling-it-quits-11655732689

Gomez, D. (2022, February 1). Why teachers are leaving and where they're going. *Forbes*. https://www.forbes.com/sites/forbescoachescouncil/2022/02/01/why-teachers-are-leaving-and-where-theyre-going/

Hoerr, T. (2009). The principal connection: Can leaders be popular? *Educational Leadership, 67*(2), 92–93.

Karns, M. (2005). Prosocial learning communities. *Leadership, 34*(5), 2–36.

Lac, V. T., Mansfield, K. C., & Fernandez, E. (2023). Working alongside students, parents, and families. *Kappan, 5*(2), 48–52. https://doi.org/10.1177/00317217231205942

McLeod, S. (2024, January 24). *Maslow's hierarchy of needs.* Simply Psychology. https://www.simplypsychology.org/maslow.htm1

National Center for Education Statistics. (2022, July 6). *More than 80 percent of U.S. public schools report pandemic has negatively impacted student behavior and socio-emotional development.* https://nces.ed.gov/whatsnew/press_releases/07_06_2022.asp

Parker, K., & Horowitz, J. M. (2022, March 9) *Majority of workers who quit a job in 2021 cite low pay, no opportunities for advancement, feeling disrespected.* Pew Research. https://www.pewresearch.org/short-reads/2022/03/09/majority-of-workers-who-quit-a-job-in-2021-cite-low-pay-no-opportunities-for-advancement-feeling-disrespected/

Pasteur, L. (n.d.). https://www.azquotes.com/quote/225935

Payne, R. (2003). *Framework for understanding poverty* (3rd ed.). Aha! Process.

Shepherd, Q., & Williamson, S. (2022). *The secret to transformational leadership.* Compassionate Leadership.

Staake, J. (2024, June 10). *2024 teacher shortage statistics show we still have a long way to go.* We Are Teachers. https://www.weareteachers.com/teacher-shortage-statistics/

Steiner, E. D., & Woo, A. (2021). *Job-related stress threatens the teacher supply: Key findings from the 2021 state of the U.S. teacher survey.* RAND. https://www.rand.org/pubs/research_reports/RRA1108-1.htm1

Surbhi, S. (2023, May 22). *Difference between faculty and staff.* Key Differences. https://keydifferences.com/difference-between-faculty-and-staff.htm1

Teacher Salary Project. (n.d.). Retrieved December 14, 2024, from https://www.teachersalaryproject.org/

Tomlinson, C. (2018). One to grow on/help teachers become master learners. *Educational Leadership, 76*(3), 1–3.

Westerfield, T. (2016). The principal factor. *Educational Leadership, 74*(1), 56–60.

Will, M. (2023a, July 4). Teachers are facing an "intentional toxic disrespect," Secretary Cardona says. *Education Week.* https://www.edweek.org/

teaching-learning/teachers-are-facing-an-intentional-toxic-disrespect-secretary-cardona-says/2023/07

Will, M. (2023b, May 22). Teachers are stressed and disrespected, but happier than last year: 7 takeaways from new poll. *Education Week.* https://www.edweek.org/teaching-learning/teachers-are-stressed-and-disrespected-but-happier-than-last-year-7-takeaways-from-new-poll/2023/05

3

Mission, Vision, and Core Values

"Okay Houston . . . we've had a problem here" (Swigert, 1970). Many of us will remember these now famous words being reported back from outer space to Mission Control in Houston, Texas. These were the words during Apollo 13's third harrowing mission to the Moon when an explosion occurred on the way, and Mission Control worked tirelessly to resolve the problem. Thinking about this event may remind us too of the movie *Apollo 13*. While the focus is usually on the astronauts and the historical significance of these events, as leaders, it is essential to remember that the people at Mission Control are managing, monitoring, and solving problems 24/7.

Knowing the mission, whether going to the moon or, for respected school leaders, the mission of educating all students, is critically important and has enormous consequences. John, a respected school leader, knows that well. Among the first things he did when he became principal over a decade ago was to ask the faculty at their first meeting if they knew the school's mission and vision. He quickly learned that no one did, despite it being posted in the school. He knew he had his work cut out for him. A school's written mission statement, as well as its written vision statement and core values, are critical to guiding and gauging a school's trajectory on a daily basis. The entire school community must be on board.

Mission

So, to begin, how do we define mission? Oxford Reference (2024) defines a mission statement as: "a formal summary of the aims and values of a company, organization, or individual." The Colorado League of Charter Schools (n.d.) defines a mission statement or mission as

> a public declaration that schools or other educational organizations use to describe their founding purpose and major organizational commitments – i.e., what they do and why they do it. A mission statement may describe a school's day-to-day operational objectives, its instrumental values, or its public commitments to students and community.

It will be helpful to look at a few school mission statements that vary in wording and length, as well as look at what our respected school leaders have done with their school mission statements to personalize and individualize them and make them come alive.

The Wilmette, Illinois, School District 39 Mission Statement states (2024):

> A Wilmette District 39 education engages, empowers, and inspires students to lead academically successful, socially responsible, compassionate, and purposeful lives. District 39 will foster a thriving learning community that cultivates growth through: Engaged Learning . . . Empowered Mindset . . . Inspired Community.

The mission statement from the Orange Public School District, in Orange, New Jersey, says (2024):

> The Orange Public School District, in collaboration with all stakeholders, is responsible for promoting the

academic, social, emotional and personal success of all students.

With a commitment to academic excellence, the district provides teachers, families, and administrators the tools needed for all students to reach their full potential.

The district serves all students in our schools, acknowledging their unique backgrounds, cultural perspectives and learning styles.

The district recognizes that curiosity, discipline, integrity, responsibility, and respect are necessary for success.

The Orange Public School District cultivates a community of 21st-century learners where students take ownership of the learning process, achieve high standards of excellence, and focus on academics.

One last mission statement is from Sunset Ridge School District 29, Northfield, Illinois (2024), which demonstrates the ease of putting a mission statement into one sentence: "Cultivating an inclusive learning community that engages hearts and minds, one child at a time."

Our four respected school leaders are principals in schools in a larger district. Each of their school districts has mission statements covering the entire district. All of the leaders have crafted a specific mission statement for their schools that supplements their district mission statement but is individualized to meet the particular needs of their schools. Three of the respected school leaders are in the Chicago Public School system, which has the following mission statement: "To provide a high quality public education for every child, in every neighborhood, that prepares each for success in college, career and civic life." To fulfill its mission, three commitments are discussed: academic progress, financial stability, and integrity. (Access the website cited in the list of references for a complete discussion.) The three respected CPS school leaders have created mission statements for their schools. Luis's school states, "The Mission of . . . is to provide our students with experiential learning through developmentally appropriate instruction that allows for individual differences and learning styles in an inclusive environment. Our school promotes a safe, orderly, and caring community that seeks to develop the whole child." Vanessa's school focuses on the fine and performing arts, and its mission statement says, "[W]e create community spaces that value and celebrate every single student, making learning rich and endless." John's school is an International Baccalaureate high school with the mission statement "Educate Global Citizens."

Our fourth respected school leader, Elena, a principal in a suburban Chicagoland school, shares her school's mission statement: "Our mission is to empower diverse, confident, and curious learners to become empathetic global leaders." Among the several schools in her district, our respected school leader's particular school is 88 percent Hispanic. She ensures that her mission statement comes alive by translating it and the vision and belief statements into Spanish so all feel welcomed and informed. Her commitment to her school's population is present in her written and spoken words (Spanish and English) and her actions. One faculty member said, "She is open to change and continually advocates for our dual[-language] students."

Odabaş and Aragão (2023) report on the content analysis and themes of 1,314 mission statements. Knowing the themes that appear in mission statements is helpful to respected school leaders creating mission statements. They state:

> These mission statements present a wide range of educational commitments and priorities. They most commonly emphasize preparing students for their futures after graduation: 80% of all mission statements mention this issue, which might include goals such as college and job readiness, developing lifelong learners, and creating productive citizens.
>
> Around two-thirds of mission statements (64%) mention the importance of providing a safe, nurturing, and healthy environment for students. Just over half (54%) mention the need for parent and community involvement in the districts' educational efforts. Somewhat smaller shares focus on the academic programs the district offers

(47%) or the importance of developing academic skills such as problem-solving or analytical and critical thinking (38%).

Other topics are far rarer. Just 12% of these documents refer to providing a student-centered education. And although parents cited mental health as a top concern in a recent survey, just 4% of mission statements explicitly mention improving the mental health of students as a core educational function.

(p. 1)

As one can see, mission statements come in all sizes, complexity and lengths as well as in the significance of the topics that are included. To gain some insight into the development of a critically needed mission statement, our four respected school leaders were asked questions about the development of their school's mission, vision, and core values. It was abundantly clear that collaboration from all stakeholders (students, teachers, administrators, parents, and the community) was essential in developing a meaningful and purposeful mission statement reflecting the school's quality and nature. There can be no rush to judgment or to get it done, and all members must be heard and acknowledged for what they bring to the table. A respected school leader takes whatever time is necessary to get everybody involved. The mission development task is team-driven, and the leader needs to ensure that the right people are on the bus. The benefits of being a respected school leader included significantly more focused engagement from stakeholders. They were empowered. Being respected as a school leader allowed participants to contribute more genuinely and meaningfully to the mission conversation. It also affirmed the respected school leader's personal beliefs. Elena stated clearly: "Being respected affirmed what I believe; I am a member of a team . . . going in the right direction."

Vision

The school's vision statement is closely aligned with its mission statement. Frequently, one will see schools and school districts stating the words *mission* and *vision* together, and occasionally, they are hard to distinguish. A. D. Obiero (n.d.) helps to clarify the difference between the two, stating, "Vision sees the stars; mission carves the path to reach them." There are key differences between a school's mission statement and its vision statement, and a respected school leader will ensure the school community understands the difference. Just like creating a mission statement, soliciting input from all community members in crafting the statement is the best place to start to ensure everyone knows them and the difference. Marymount University (2023) helps us to understand the difference between them by stating,

> The primary difference between a mission statement and a vision statement is that a mission statement describes the school's current and/or founding identity and the key values that characterize the school as it is in the present. A vision statement, on the other hand, looks forward to the future.

Paul C. Young (2023) shares another view of the difference in his article "Finding Your School's Mission and Vision." He states that a mission represents why a school exists and its fundamental purpose, such as teaching, whereas a vision is the method for accomplishing goals.

Finally, Skrabanek (2024) states: "The *mission statement* focuses on today and what the organization does to achieve it. The *vision statement* focuses on tomorrow and what the organization wants to become."

Navigating mission and vision statements can be complex and challenging. School leaders, especially beginning ones who have plenty on their plates with the daily challenges of leading schools, may barely have enough time to realize that a mission and vision statement exist. They know in their hearts what they believe and what the school needs to accomplish, but actual statements may not be brought to mind even when posted in several places throughout the school, as John, one of our respected school leaders, noted. However, respected school leaders like John knew that was the first place he had to start, the first order of business. As it has been said, if you don't know where you are going, you will never know if you have gotten there. Knowing a school's vision statement is critical in providing all school employees with a road map for collaborative partnership and a mechanism for gauging progress and goal attainment. Everyone in the school should know the school's vision statement and mission statement and should be able to state it or, if it's too long, summarize it. What sets a respected school leader apart from others is that the respected school leader ensures that this happens because, as they say, that is where the rubber meets the road.

A few vision statements will be helpful here.

The Weston, Massachusetts, public schools (n.d.) states its vision statement in three sentences as follows:

> Weston Public Schools and the wider school community are committed to multiple pathways toward excellence and achievement for all students. Students will imagine, reflect, and innovate within a safe, equitable, and responsive learning environment that develops their academic, social, and emotional growth and holistic well-being. Students will develop the critical thinking, creative problem solving, technological and media literacy, communication, and collaboration skills necessary for civic engagement and lifelong learning.

Some schools have developed a vision statement in one sentence. The Deer Park Public Schools (n.d.) in Cincinnati, Ohio, is an excellent example, declaring the district as a "high-performing district that prepares our students to be critical thinkers and problem solvers and to live a life of purpose and impact."

The San Francisco Unified School District (n.d.) discusses its vision statement with a decade-plus expectation "for what SFUSD students will know and be able to do" as follows:

> All SFUSD students will graduate as independent thinkers with a sense of agency who have attained academic and creative skills to lead productive lives and contribute to our community.

Vision statements, like mission statements, come in different formats and are carefully crafted for each district and/or school. Once again, our three CPS respected school leaders took the CPS district vision statement and then each individualized it to their particular schools. The CPS vision statement states "Success Starts Here" and includes its core values of student-centered, whole child, equity, academic excellence, community partnership, and continuous learning. (Core values as a separate topic will be discussed later in this chapter.) As a district, CPS ensures that those core values are "adhered to in all of our planning and practices." Specific, detailed, and measurable five-year goals are enumerated in striving to achieve the district's vision. Please see the CPS website for significantly more details.

Our three CPS respected school leaders' vision statements were crafted to supplement CPS's (n.d.) lengthy, detailed vision statement and represent each leader's school with its idiosyncrasies. For example, the vision statement crafted at Luis's elementary school states the vision is "to develop leaders who strive for academic excellence, social awareness, and emotional intelligence, all while instilling in them critical thinking skills, a global perspective, and a respect for core values." The vision statement for Vanessa's school states that it

> strives for "Excellence Through Perseverance" to meet the academic, social, and emotional needs of all students, including diverse learners and their learning needs, by implementing research-based instruction on various "Learning Modalities."
>
> We believe rigor allows us to use differentiated strategies incorporated throughout our curriculum to support the unique learning needs of all students. We believe, against all odds, all students have the ability to persevere.

Finally, John's school keeps it simple so everyone can quickly memorize it and repeat it if asked. It says, "Create a Better World."

Our fourth respected school leader, Elena, has a district vision statement "to inspire a passion for learning in every child." Elena worked with her school community to develop a vision statement specific to her school. It reads, "Our vision, as a dual language school, is to foster a community that provides safe, authentic learning that is inclusive for all students to empower their identities, cultivate curiosity, develop creative solutions, and promote a sense of global responsibility."

All our respected school leaders have carefully crafted individual vision statements to supplement and support their district's vision statement and make their schools come alive. It is essential to note the importance of having all stakeholders involved and being a leader/listener who can hear everyone. Our respected school leader John clearly emphasizes the importance of a vision statement and listening carefully to all stakeholders. His words are powerful. He says,

> I do listen differently to every stakeholder. I believe people need to understand what I learned years ago. Schools are essential nonprofit businesses, but they are different than businesses. A corporation and a school are both businesses. However, if a corporation was a zebra and a school was a horse, if you squint your eyes, they both look the same, however they are vastly different. I have a Master of Education in Business and a Master of Educational Leadership. In business the objective is clear. Maximize owners' equity and make a profit. Everyone in the business knows this and everyone understands this is OUR priority and everyone should hopefully buy into that vision. In a school setting there are hundreds if not thousands of objectives. . . . I like to think the respect I have earned can focus everyone on the fact that we are all here for all of our students. When I am listening to someone I need to first and foremost make them feel heard but more silently and skillfully bring them to a point where at least part of their motivation is in alignment with what's best for all of our students. . . . The benefit comes when you can get everyone to see that they all have a common goal. When that happens, it is my experience to try to facilitate communication between all the parties involved and then get out of the way because

when you have motivated people with a common cause that involves what's best for kids, good stuff happens.

Our respected school leader Luis, relates the importance of everyone being on a team, working in unison, and heading in the right direction. He states, "School mission, vision, and core values are driven by a team, ensuring you have the right people on the team. People can stay on the train, get off the train, or switch seats." Our respected school leader Vanessa states that when you are respected, there will be more engagement on the part of stakeholders. Lastly, Elena shared that one must have a shared vision for learning that everyone supports. She stated that the pandemic gave her "the time and opportunity to listen to everyone individually" and discuss the shared vision for learning.

As one can see, vision statements come in various forms and complexity, like mission statements. Roland Barth (1993), the founding director of the Principals Center and former senior lecturer on education at the Harvard University Graduate School of Education, stated, "A school with a vigorous, soaring vision of what it might become is more likely to become that; without a vision, a school is unlikely to improve." He continues, "For me, a vision is a kind of moral imagination which gives school people, individually and collectively, the ability to see their school not only as it is, but as they would like it to become." He offers the following nine ways to create a vision: inherit a vision, explicate a vision, refine a vision, borrow a vision, buy a vision, inflict a vision, fire a vision/hire a vision, homogenize a vision, and grow a vision.

It was clear from our respected school leaders that "growing a vision" together with representation from the entire school community is the best way to create a long-lasting vision that will be remembered and used in schools' daily lives. Larry Lashway (1997), author of *Leading With a Vision*, makes two important points about the importance of a school leader leading the task of creating a vision.

1. *Developing a vision does not necessarily begin with a formal, highly publicized statement.* It **does** begin with a leader who

relentlessly seeks to keep the school moving forward – often in small ways – whenever opportunity knocks. Such leaders seem to be guided by a deep sense of personal values; however, they do not always package these as an explicit vision, and they remain open to the ideas of others.
2. *Developing a vision is not a neat, linear process with clear beginnings and steady progress toward the goal.* There are times to steam ahead, times to back off, and times to take a detour. In short, visionary principals seem to have the passion of revolutionaries but the patient pragmatism of moderates.

His book is replete with ideas on developing a vision and how the school leader is the guardian of that vision. The concept of *guardian* or *keeper* of the vision has a critical place in the day-to-day life of schools, particularly for schools that work toward diversity, equity, and inclusion. While a later chapter of this book is dedicated to this topic, it is worth noting here that a research study conducted by Brad Kose (2011) concluded that the findings "delineate principals' practices in developing a transformative vision and suggest several useful dimensions of transformative vision statements." Transformative leadership emphasizes equity, diversity, social justice, and fighting oppression. A carefully crafted vision statement can greatly benefit moving the needle on these critical issues.

Burt Nanus (1992), author of *Visionary Leadership*, summarizes the criticality and benefits of having a vision. "The right vision attracts commitment and energizes people. The right vision creates meaning in workers' lives. The right vision establishes a standard of excellence. The right vision bridges the present to the future." Nanus's book was intended for business leaders, but the benefits apply to educational leadership.

Respected school leaders know the significance of having an achievable vision for their schools. As stated, if we don't know where we are going, we will never know if we get there. It is important to monitor that vision and what has been done to implement it. As Vanessa's faculty members stated,

She is a strong, good principal.

She is an effective leader.

I feel it takes at least three years to see the effectiveness of a leader and to see if the systems and procedures that the leader has implemented are working accordingly. Also, it allows people to see how the leader has changed what needs to be adjusted to the operations and systems that were first implemented.

One must ensure that once a vision is in place, it is not lost in translation or over time. The respected school leader can make a difference in developing the vision statement and ensuring it is lived every day, in school life and in planning sessions, such as curriculum work, strategic planning, and administrative and governing board meetings.

John has always been a "vision" person, a perfect trait for a principal. When presented with almost any situation (student issue, teacher issue, parent issue), John is always mindful that whatever we decide to do helps all parties involved progress along a positive, sustainable growth path. John's faculty member said it well: "Mr. J. is a visionary with a big heart."

In education, there is a honeymoon, a trial, and/or a forgiving/lenient phase, often given when there is a new principal. A higher level of awareness or reality follows this. Soon, the principal adjusts and becomes familiar with the staff and the student body. Here, in this second phase, there is an opportunity to develop trust, open-mindedness to ideas (former and current), and humility or acceptance of assistance. Hopefully, the principal's vision and mission will stay constant; however, a plan may need to be altered to get all faculty on board and reach all students.

Core Values

Carefully aligned to a school's mission and vision statements are its core values. A school's core values work in harmony with its mission and vision to make the school what it is and shape what it hopes to become. At first glance, the term *core values* may seem easy to define. What comes to mind when you think of the word *core*? The word is used frequently in our vernacular, and thinking about its multiple uses helps define and validate the critical importance of "core" in core values. Cores are found in many contexts, such as the Earth, nuclear reactors, apples, baseballs, and the human body. Sometimes, it describes how you might feel: shaken to the core.

However, the first of these connotations, the Earth's core, specifically its inner core, is particularly intense and revealing concerning the possible profound nature when using the word *core*. According to the California Academy of Sciences (n.d.):

> The innermost part of Earth is the core, which is about 1,500 miles (2414 km) thick. Both the inner and outer cores consist primarily of iron and nickel. They're extremely hot, ranging from 7200–9000°F (4000–5000°C). The inner core is under intense pressure, which keeps it solid despite high temperatures.

Thinking of the intensity of the word *core* here helps when using it with core values and highlights the critical importance of core values in a school.

Respected school leaders know they must have a set of easy-to-understand written core values that all school community members understand. Robyn K. Jackson (2020), in "Co-Creating Your School's Core Values," clearly defines core values. She states:

> A school's core values are terms of practice that clearly define how everyone will work together to achieve the school's vision and carry out its mission. Core values are not aspirations, and they are not self-congratulatory; they are practical. They tell a school staff, "This is how we need to behave, and this is what we need to do to live out our mission and achieve our vision." To generate core values that are powerful and useful, make them non-negotiable and get everyone's buy-in.

As with the vision and mission statements, showing some school district core value statements will be helpful here.

Glenview School District 34, Glenview, Illinois, posts the following as its core values (n.d.): growth and aspirations; diversity, inclusion, and equity; relationships and respect; and stewardship. Each core value is detailed and can be found on the district's website.

The Cherry Creek School District (2023), Greenwood Village, Colorado, has the following five core values:

> *The Cherry Creek School District is dedicated to kids and grounded in a belief that every student can succeed and achieve a bright future.* Through conversations with our community over the past two years, we've identified five core values that guide our work and help every student find a pathway to a fulfilling future. Those five core values – Equity, Growth Mindset, Whole Wellbeing, Relationships, and Engagement – are the grounding force for empowering every student with what we call a Pathway of Purpose.

Lastly, one more example, from the Rochester Community Schools (n.d.), Rochester, Michigan, is valuable here:

> The educational foundation at Virtual Campus is built on six Core Values: adventure, community, internationalism, agency, innovation, and personalization. Reflective of best practice research from Harvard Graduate School of Education, MIT, Stanford, and Teacher's College amongst others, the Core Values provide a common language shared by all educators on campus. With these ideas in mind, our VC faculty design educational opportunities and participate together as a community of thinkers and learners.

Core values clarify and crystalize what is important and cherished in a district and/or school. A look at our respected school leaders will help shed additional light. As noted, three of our respected school leaders are in the Chicago Public Schools. CPS (n.d.) has an extended section on its website regarding core values, with much discussion regarding an intent to have its core values "adhered to in all of our planning and practices." The six core values are student-centered, whole child, equity, academic excellence, community partnership, and continuous learning.

The three respected school leaders adhere to these core values in their daily practice. Luis specifically mentions core values in his school's personalized vision statement. He notes that the vision is to have "respect for core values."

On the other hand, some schools use belief statements to define what is valued in their schools. Elena's district has seven belief statements, including the following three, which she frequently reflects upon as a respected school leader:

> We believe in utilizing innovative instructional practices that encourage collaboration, creativity, and exploration.
>
> We believe in student-centered classrooms and schools that are supportive, safe, and responsive to the social and emotional needs of students, staff, and families.
>
> We believe in creating and maintaining a culture where students and staff learn from each other, share ideas, and build supportive, collaborative relationships.

She said, "I hope my legacy is that what I did is what they [the school community] needed. I am here to make a change that everybody needs and that is aligned with our mission, vision, and values that we developed over time."

Concerning core values as well as mission and vision and, well, "everything" about her school, one of Vanessa's faculty members stated,

> My principal pays attention to everything in the school. She is very kind and has a big heart and understands what is going with her staff. She makes decisions based on the whole school's needs, which could benefit everyone [school staff, parents, and students]. That is what I liked

Mission, Vision, and Core Values ◆ 55

most about her [being fair to everybody]. She lends her ears to everyone and knows how to consider our comments. My principal is really one of a kind!

Core values indeed come into play when one of Luis's community members stated,

> I appreciate our principal's advocacy for his students and staff. He is not afraid to challenge issues. This year we received a high number of refugee students and he has embraced the students and families with open arms and has worked on making them feel welcomed in our school community.

Lastly, two parents in John's school community commented on his attributes and personal characteristics, which are closely aligned with core values. One said, "[John's] empathy shows through every conversation or meeting I've had with him." The other parent went into great detail and stated:

> We have been at the school since 7th grade. Our family enrolled during the most difficult time of our family life as we faced homelessness and a terminal illness with my husband. The principal and assistant principal have been with us every step.
>
> We often say it's a top-down approach in the administrative corporate world. This means that the top leader leads, and the rest follow. [John] is an excellent leader. He cares about the students and his staff. He finds solutions to problems. He celebrates achievements and milestones that his students and staff achieve. He does not hold onto any "keys to success." He shares his knowledge and always encourages each student to do their best.
>
> Jimmy was having a tough time during Covid. I mentioned it via email to my principal, and a couple of days later, a [school] sweatshirt came in the mail for him. He cares.

Just like mission and vision statements, core value statements can be sketched in many ways, but they all have one thing in common: they get to the heart (the core!) of what the school stands for. The key is having statements created under the guidance of a respected school leader that are forged by representatives from the entire school community. Everyone should be aware of the statements, practice them daily, advocate for them, cultivate them, and help perpetuate their sustainability. Developing long-lasting mission, vision, and core values must be part of a school's strategic plan.

Lauren Kaufman and Chris Hartigan (2024) wrote that there are six ideas that "our district employs to create a culture of mentoring and coaching in our leadership team. By embracing these actionable strategies, leaders can bridge connections, enhance relationships, and ignite meaningful professional dialogue." The first strategy was to "embody the district mission and vision." They further state:

> Crafting a mission and vision statement is a collaborative endeavor that engages various stakeholders, including students, teachers, building and district leadership, parents, and community members. This inclusive process should illuminate core values, beliefs, and goals through strategic planning, fostering a shared commitment to the organization's purpose and direction. Leaders should make these statements visible throughout an organization and use them to guide their actions. The National Policy Board for Educational Administration's professional standards for education leaders are a valuable resource when reflecting on your district's mission and vision.

Another actionable strategy is to "connect core values."

It is important to note here that the respected school leader model to be discussed in a later chapter uses the National Policy Board for Educational Administration's (2015) 10 Professional Standards for Educational Leaders (PSEL) as the first of two bedrock pieces of the respected school leader model. The first of 10 standards discussed in detail is the school's mission, vision, and core values.

Case Study

Our respected school leader John, worked tirelessly when he first came to his school more than a decade ago to get the entire school community on board with developing and implementing a vision and mission statement aligned with his International Baccalaureate high school. While he already had CPS's vision, mission, and core values statements, he went further. He said:

> The first thing I did was to ask everyone I saw in the school, "What is our vision and mission statement?" I was really not surprised when no one knew it or even knew how to find it. At our first teacher meeting in 2019, I held up a 100-dollar bill and told the 300 staff members, this is yours if you can stand up and tell me our mission or vision statement. No one stood up. Everyone started to open Google on their phones, and I said, "Please stop." The fact of the matter is I did not know the statement. I found it on our website, but it was three paragraphs long and had far too many overused educational words, like *pedagogy, 21st-century learner, best practice*, and *rigor*. It was terrible. It reminded me of my daughter when I would allow her to dress herself when she was five: Too much stuff and nothing matched. I was a big fan of the companies that had short mission and vision statements. Google: "To organize the world's information and make it universally accessible and useful." Tesla: "To accelerate the world's transition to sustainable energy." Microsoft: "To empower every person and every organization on the planet to achieve more." Our new mission and vision statement would be concise and to the point. It would pinpoint exactly what we

do every day for every student. It would be exactly seven words long: Educate Global Citizens. Create a Better World.

Then, at one of my meetings that year, I held up a bill in my hand, and before I could say anything, teachers stood up and said, "Educate Global Citizens to Create a Better World." I said, "You win . . . the one dollar I have in my hand." There was a collective groan followed by a chuckle.

[John then answered this question:] How have you benefited from knowing you are respected for fulfilling your school's mission, vision, and core values?

I say with some pride that our mission and vision statement is known by a higher percentage of our staff than in any other school. It adorns many of our hallways, and this simple message always keeps us focused when plans need to be made. I ask you right now: Do you know what your school's mission and vision statement is by heart?

Reflection Questions:

Q1 If surveyed, what do you think your students, faculty, parents, and school community members would say about your leadership in developing and living your school's mission, vision, and core values?

Q2 How have your mission, vision, and core values affected your students?

Q3 How do you, as a respected school leader, live your school's mission and vision and model your school's core values daily?

References

Barth, R. (1993). Coming to a vision. *Journal of Staff Development, 14*(1), 6–11.

California Academy of Sciences. (n.d.). *From core to crust: Defining Earth's layers*. Retrieved July 3, 2024, from https://www.calacademy.org/explore-science/from-core-to-crust-defining-earths-layers

Cherry Creek Schools. (2023). *About us*. https://www.cherrycreekschools.org/Page/14311

Chicago Public Schools. (n.d.). *Our vision*. Retrieved July 2, 2024, from https://www.cps.edu/globalassets/cps-pages/about-cps/vision/resources-page/vision19_onepager_english.pdf

Colorado League of Charter Schools. (n.d.). *Mission, vision, and school culture: New schools guide*. Retrieved July 2, 2024, from https://www.cde.state.co.us/cdechart/newschoolworkbookbootcamp

Deer Park Community City School District. (n.d.). *About*. Retrieved July 3, 2024, from https://www.deerparkcityschools.org/about/mission-and-vision-statements

Glenview School District 34. (n.d.). *Strategic plan: 2024–2027*. Retrieved July 3, 2024, from https://www.glenview34.org/d34-at-a-glance/strategic-plan

Jackson, R. K. (2020). Co-creating your school's core values. *Educational Leadership, 62*(12).

Kaufman, L., & Hartigan, C. (2024, June 4). How principals can be mentors rather than just superiors: 6 strategies for leading your school with a coaching lens. *Education Week*. https://www.edweek.org/leadership/opinion-how-principals-can-be-mentors-rather-than-just-superiors/2024/06

Kose, B. (2011). Developing a transformative school vision: Lessons from peer-nominated principals. *Education and Urban Society, 43*(2), 119–136. https://doi.org/10.1177/0013124510380231

Lashway, L. (1997). *Leading with a vision*. ERIC Clearinghouse on Educational Management.

Marymount University. (2023, February 16). *How to write school mission and vision statements*. https://online.marymount.edu/blog/how-write-school-mission-and-vision-statements

Nanus, B. (1992). *Visionary leadership*. Jossey-Bass.

National Policy Board for Educational Administration. (2015). *Professional standards for educational leaders.* National Policy Board for Educational Administration.

Obiero, A. D. (n.d.). Retrieved July 2, 2024, from https://www.goodreads.com/quotes/tag/mission-quotes

Odabaş, M., & Aragão, C. (2023, April 4). *School district mission statements highlight a partisan divide over diversity, equity, and inclusion in K-12 education.* Pew Research Center. https://www.pewresearch.org/social-trends/2023/04/04/school-district-mission-statements-highlight-a-partisan-divide-over-diversity-equity-and-inclusion-in-k-12-education/

Orange Public Schools. (2024). *Vision and mission statements.* https://www.orange.k12.nj.us/domain/3183

Oxford Reference. (2024). *Mission.* https://www.oxfordreference.com/display/10.1093/oi/authority.20110826110258868

Rochester Community Schools. (n.d.). *Our core values.* Retrieved July 3, 2024, from https://virtualcampus.rochester.k12.mi.us/about/our-core-values

San Francisco Unified School District. (n.d.). *About the vision, values, goals, and guardrails.* Retrieved July 3, 2024, from https://www.sfusd.edu/about-sfusd/our-mission-and-vision

Skrabanek, B. (2024, June 4). *Difference between mission and vision statements: 25 examples.* ClearVoice. https://www.clearvoice.com/resources/difference-between-mission-vision-statement-examples/

Sunset Ridge School District 29. (2024). *Strategic plans.* https://sunsetridge29.org/13616_4

Swigert, J. (1970, April 14). *Apollo 13: "Houston, we've had a problem"* [Video]. YouTube. https://www.youtube.com/watch?v=MdvoA-sjs0A

Weston Massachusetts Public Schools. (n.d.). *Vision statement.* Retrieved July 3, 2024, from https://www.westonschools.org/district/vision-statement/

Wilmette Public Schools District 39. (2024). *Mission statement.* https://wilmette39.ss9.sharpschool.com/about_d39/mission_statement

Young, P. G. (2023, November 8). *Finding your school's mission and vision.* Edutopia. https://www.edutopia.org/article/forming-schools-vision-mission-statements/

4

School Culture and Climate

As you walk into your school, can you describe the culture and climate of your school? Can you feel it? Can you take the daily climate and culture temperature? Can you tell if the culture and climate are positive or negative? Do you know the difference between school culture and school climate? According to Fullan (2008), a school principal directly affects the school culture positively or negatively. He argues that principals in today's educational organizations need to focus on more than just high achievement and standards. The focus for the principal, Fullan (2002) states, must be on creating long-lasting and sustainable culture change.

What you see on the walls, how you are greeted by faculty, and the interaction among faculty and students are all signs of the culture and climate in the school. It's what you see and feel when you first walk into the school building. The culture and climate of a school play a critical role in shaping the overall educational experience and outcomes for students, teachers, and the school community. The ultimate goal of a respected school leader is to cultivate a positive school culture and climate where teachers and students feel safe and learning is at the core. As John Maxwell (2022, p. 86) stated, "When people respect you as a person, they admire you. When they respect you as a friend, they love you. When they respect you as a leader, they follow you."

The culture and climate of a school are complex and have multifaceted aspects that significantly influence the overall educational experience of students, teachers, parents, and staff. While the terms *culture* and *climate* are often used interchangeably by many leaders, they encompass different aspects of the school environment and student experiences. School culture and climate are not physical material that we can reach out and touch, but they are still something that students, staff, and visitors can identify and feel. How do we define school culture and climate? What is the difference?

Culture Definition

The importance of school culture cannot be overstated, but what is school culture? Gruenert and Whitaker (2015) define culture as "the social glue that holds people together" (p. 6). School culture is more permanent and built over time, reflecting the school's prevailing traditions, shared values, rules, and beliefs. These belief patterns and practices shape the way members of the school community interact with one another and approach teaching and learning (Cakiroglu et al., 2012). It is the underlying philosophy or personality of the school. According to Gordana (2020), school culture can and often is observed through the lens of culture in general. Just as a group of people belonging to the same culture shares core beliefs, values, and assumptions, so does a school community. All members of the school community comprise the school culture. The culture in a school includes norms, unwritten rules, traditions, and expectations, and these may vary among individual schools. You could identify a school's culture by the language and behavior the teachers, staff, and students use toward each other. For example, a school with a positive culture may create a welcoming, inclusive, and collaborative environment. These may also influence the way faculty dress, the way they interact with each other, and their overall professional behavior (Deal & Peterson, 1999).

The culture of a school is critical as it shapes the environment in which students learn and grow. Fostering a healthy culture is the foundation of a school's progress and success. When students feel connected to their school community, supported by teachers and peers, and guaranteed safety in their environment, they are more likely to perform better academically and be motivated to succeed (Starkey, 2023). Teachers also thrive in an environment where they feel valued and supported. When a respected school leader promotes collaboration among teachers, allowing them to share ideas, resources, and strategies that benefit student learning, teachers feel respected, and morale increases. A school with a healthy culture will have established clear expectations for behavior. It will promote empathy, inclusivity, support for students' emotional well-being, and respectful interactions among students and staff. This leads to improved student behavior and reduced disciplinary issues and can contribute to overall growth (Gray et al., 2017).

School culture goes beyond academics, rules, and routines because it creates a nurturing and supportive environment where every person in the school feels valued and can thrive academically, socially, and emotionally. A respected school leader can create a healthy school culture to set the foundation for lifelong learning. In this environment, students and teachers can learn important life skills such as teamwork, resilience, and leadership. These skills are essential for success in future endeavors, whether in higher education, careers, or personal life.

While school culture primarily involves what lies beneath the surface, there are elements of it that are visible. According to Schein's (2010) model of organizational culture, there are three levels of culture. The first level is artifacts, the symbols we see in the hallways, showcases, and classrooms, students' work, mementos, and accomplishments that demonstrate pride in the community and its members. Information regarding learning initiatives, the mission and vision of the school, and policies and procedures of the school are also artifacts. As you enter many schools today, you will see a television or monitor displaying pictures of the students involved in events that they are proud of and images of the school's mission and vision. As you walk through the halls at respected school leader John's high school, you notice the presence of the International Baccalaureate (IB) program they offer. The IB program is designed to develop well-rounded students with the knowledge, skills, dispositions, and sense of purpose to respond to today's challenges with optimism and an open mind and make the world a better place (IB, n.d.). The IB program is a program that the school community is proud to offer many of their students. As IB learners, they strive to be balanced, caring communicators, inquirers, knowledgeable, open-minded, principled, reflective, risk-takers, and thinkers, and these words are hung on banners throughout the halls. As IB learners, these are the traits they strive to embody every day, and their mission is to develop internationally minded people who recognize their common humanity and shared guardianship of the planet and help to create a better and more peaceful world (IB, n.d.).

The second level Schein (2010) describes is espoused values that drive students, teachers, and the community in their work. The values of the individuals working in the school play a critical role in defining the school's culture. One faculty member at Elena's school describes her as a "risk-taker leader" who often takes chances on the teachers in the building. Many of the teachers at her school feel she trusts their opinions and the strategies they choose to use in their classrooms and believe they have the skills required to do their job. The teachers in Elena's building feel supported, and according to one teacher, this "drives and inspires them to be innovative leaders" in their classrooms and the school. When teachers feel supported and trusted by their school leaders, it helps to create a positive mindset about their work. These values are the unseen but influential parts of the school culture. Schein (2010) believes that the individual's mindset associated with any organization influences the culture of the workplace.

The third level that Schein (2010) suggests is assumptions. Perhaps this is the most crucial element of school culture, the assumptions the community has about every member and aspect of that community. According to several parents, John is a respected school leader in his community because, they say, "He is very effective in leading his staff and students. He is professional; he has an open-door policy and cares about his staff, students, and families in his community." Schein (2010) argues that for school leaders to deepen their understanding of culture and create a positive school culture in their school, they need to dig deeper into the underlying assumptions, such as the mission and vision of the school. School leaders need to understand how culture exists within the walls of their schools.

Climate Definition

School climate refers to the "quality and character of the school life" (National School Climate Center, 2007, p. 5), including the physical, emotional, and social aspects of the school environment and how they affect students, staff, and the broader community. School climate is all about the visible, practical aspects of a school and how it's managed. It is more than one individual's experience; instead, it is the overall atmosphere or feeling in a school. When John was asked about the climate in his school, he stated, "Ever since we've been on the radar of other schools in the state and the country, we have had our share of visitors. When they walk our hallways, they comment on how friendly our students are and how they always say hello." School climate is a building block of school culture; a good teacher is just one person on a successful team (Kane et al., 2016).

School climate sets the tone for the entire educational experience. It includes the attitudes, values, norms, and relationships that shape daily interactions in the school community. A positive school climate improves academic outcomes, supports students' holistic development, and contributes to a thriving and inclusive learning environment. Therefore, nurturing and maintaining a positive school climate is essential for the overall success and well-being of everyone in the school.

School principals are vital in setting the tone of the school climate. They play an important role in fostering relationships, creating a positive framework, commending successes, and hiring the right staff. Elena's school's primary language is Spanish; however, they foster relationships in their community by welcoming all languages. The materials that are distributed to the community are required to be in both English and Spanish. The faculty and staff often comment on her "kindness" as a respected school leader. This sets the tone for the faculty and staff and how they treat those who enter the school. When Elena was asked about how her faculty and staff treat people who enter her school, she commented, "The faculty and staff are incredibly kind people," and this helps create a positive climate. They cultivate a positive environment by truly believing that their students and parents should feel important. Elena and her faculty believe in "collective responsibility" at every meeting and event that happens in the school.

Although "school culture" and "school climate" are related, they refer to distinct or different aspects of the school environment. School culture represents a school's deeply rooted, long-term traits, while school climate reflects the current perceptions and experiences of the school community. Both elements are crucial in shaping a school's overall educational environment and student outcomes.

Societal Changes Affecting School Culture and Climate

Each school has a unique culture and climate identified, shaped, and nurtured by all its stakeholders. However, additional factors influence a school's culture and climate. When school leaders understand and manage these factors, they help foster a positive and supportive school culture and climate that enhances learning and the well-being of all members of the school community.

A few examples of factors that can influence or affect a school's culture are the relationships and interactions among teachers, administrators, and other staff members (staff dynamics); the level of engagement and support from parents and the wider community (community and parental involvement); shared values, norms, beliefs, and expectations among stakeholders; and school traditions, ceremonies, and rituals that can strengthen a positive school culture and create a sense of community.

Climate is also affected by a variety of factors, such as the quality of teaching, curriculum, and educational programs that can contribute positively or negatively (teaching and learning); the condition of facilities, cleanliness, safety, and aesthetics of the school building and grounds (physical environment); school policies regarding discipline, inclusivity, respect, and academic expectations (policies and practices); and physical and emotional safety as well as the support for students' well-being (safety and well-being). Factors that can significantly affect a school's overall culture and climate are the attitudes, behaviors, and priorities of school leaders and how information is shared and communicated. Socioeconomic factors, community issues, and broader societal trends, such as a tax referendum, can influence the school's culture and climate.

The culture and climate in schools have undergone various societal changes in recent years. This has been influenced by shifts in societal values, advancements in technology, focus on students' mental health and safety, using more student-centered approaches to teaching, creating partnerships with parents, including environmental education into the curriculum, evolving educational policies, and broader cultural trends, such as diversity, equity, and inclusion (DEI) in schools. These societal changes have manifested in schools in several ways. There is a growing emphasis on creating inclusive school environments that celebrate diversity (such as ethnic, cultural, linguistic, and socioeconomic). Schools increasingly promote cultural awareness, equity, and acceptance among students and staff.

The widespread adoption of technology has transformed classrooms, making learning more accessible, interactive, and personalized. Technologies such as online platforms and collaboration tools facilitate communication and strengthen relationships between students, teachers, and parents. These platforms can promote a collaborative culture where information sharing and teamwork are valued. Technology has created new ways of communicating and learning among students and teachers. It endows our students with readiness and adaptability and equips them with the essential skills they need for the digital world and future workforce. Technology can bridge gaps by providing equal access to resources and fostering an inclusive culture where all students have an equal opportunity to learn and succeed.

Technology can also have a negative effect on students in school. Students can become easily distracted due to easy access to social media, games, and entertainment on digital devices. Constant notifications and online stimuli can make it challenging for students to maintain attention and focus. Excessive screen time can lead to sleep deprivation and health issues for some students. Easy access to technology can lead to cyberbullying and online safety concerns. Respected school leaders implement balanced technology policies and digital literacy education programs and support teachers in creating strategies to promote healthy technology use and ensure student well-being.

There is a greater focus on the importance of mental health in academic success. Respected school leaders increasingly focus on creating supportive environments that address students' emotional well-being through counseling services, mindfulness programs, and initiatives to reduce stress and anxiety. Many of Elena's students commented on how she interacts with students positively. One student stated, "I love the way my principal is always so kind no matter what is going on. She always tries her best to have our school and students be as good as possible." What creates a nurturing environment is positive interactions between students and adults in the school. These interactions affect the mental health of the students.

Schools are hyper-aware of the safety concerns of their students and staff. The multiple school shootings across the United States have compelled school leaders to improve safety measures and implement stricter security protocols to bolster school safety. This includes measures such as active shooter drills, security and surveillance systems, metal detectors, and policies to prevent bullying and harassment.

Traditional teaching methods have been moving toward more student-centered approaches that prioritize critical thinking, problem-solving, and collaborative learning. One student stated about his principal (John), "He is amazing and approachable. He is very student-centered, and he trusts his teachers and leads with positivity." Student-centered approaches will better prepare our students for the rapidly changing world and workforce they will encounter.

Respected school leaders recognize the importance of partnerships with parents and the broader community. Parents at

John's school feel he is consistent with weekly outreach to families in their community. Collaboration between the school, families, and community organizations is essential for supporting student success and holistic development.

The integration of environmental education into the schools' curricula is increasing. This includes teaching sustainability practices, promoting eco-friendly behaviors, and raising awareness about climate change and its global implications. These changes reflect broader societal shifts and evolving educational philosophies to create more inclusive, supportive, and engaging learning environments for all students.

Creating/Cultivating a Positive School Culture and Climate

What do you think of when you think of an excellent school? Outstanding academics? For sure! A variety of teaching techniques? Yes! However, a positive school culture and climate are equally important and are not usually mentioned when discussing what makes an excellent school. Research shows that a school's culture and climate influence how students learn, and the respected school leader plays a pivotal role in shaping and supporting a school's culture and climate. Respected school leaders cultivate an environment where all community members feel safe, have a sense of belonging, feel respected, and are motivated to learn and grow. Students who don't feel safe and respected have trouble concentrating and learning can be difficult. When students feel like they belong to a school community, they have higher self-esteem and are more resilient and happier.

A school with a positive school culture led by a respected school leader has policies addressing bullying, harassment, diversity, equity, and inclusion. However, policies are not enough. The best way to find out about the culture of a school is to talk to the students and watch how they act and interact in the school. Do students look happy? Do they feel at home? Do they feel comfortable voicing their ideas? You will witness celebrations and acceptance of all students: the studious, the athlete, the musician, and the artist. There is a culture of acceptance and appreciation of everyone in the school. Schools with a positive culture have low rates of substance abuse, bullying, suspensions, and absenteeism and higher academic achievement and psychosocial well-being (Great Schools, 2020).

Respected school leaders can support a positive school culture by articulating a clear vision for their desired culture and climate. This vision should be communicated consistently and effectively to all stakeholders. As role models for behavior and attitudes, the respected school leader should demonstrate the values they expect from students and staff, such as respect, inclusivity, and a commitment to learning. Creating and sustaining a positive school culture and climate are critical for fostering a supportive and conducive learning environment where students can thrive academically, socially, and emotionally. As a respected school leader, Elena values being supportive and welcoming. The culture in her school is "everyone should be seen, heard, and feel important."

The principal's influence extends beyond administrative tasks and directly affects the school community's attitudes, behaviors, and relationships. When principals encourage open dialogue and are transparent in their communication with students, parents, and staff, they foster trust and collaboration. John spends time each day in the dean's office and his office counseling students one on one. He is not afraid to share with his students the mistakes he has made, how he took the road less traveled, and most importantly, how he overcame many of life's obstacles. "My honesty, open-mindedness, and willingness to help my students is the best work I do," he says. He creates an honest and trustworthy culture and connection with his students by being supportive, caring, and compassionate.

Respected school leaders need to provide opportunities for staff to learn about and contribute to improving school culture and climate. They should provide ongoing professional development that includes training on topics such as conflict resolution, cultural competency, and fostering a safe and positive school culture and climate. They should create a sense of belonging and an environment where everyone feels safe from bullying, harassment, and discrimination. This environment recognizes and celebrates achievements related to improving school culture and climate. The respected school leader reinforces positive behaviors and encourages ongoing efforts.

Using Data

Respected school leaders use data, such as surveys and discipline records, to assess the current climate and track progress over time. Data can help guide decision-making and identify areas needing improvement. When principals support positive change, it is important that they involve all stakeholders in the decision-making process. Habegger (2008) explains how her quest to answer the question "So, how does a principal get past the 'daily survival mode' to create a successful learning environment?" led her to study the role of a principal in schools. A key component explored was how principals nurtured a culture where each individual felt valued. Habegger (2008) discovered what each of the principals was doing differently and stated, "The answer lies with the school culture – principals need to create a positive school culture that promotes learning and engagement for students and adults." Creating a positive school culture is an intentional decision made by the principal. Luis intentionally sets the tone each morning at his school with the "Morning Mantra," saying The United States pledge of allegiance, and "Get ready to learn!" He does this routine when he is off-site as well. He knows how important it is for his students to hear his voice. He has intentionally decided to create a positive school culture where students know adults are here to help them learn.

Use Collaboration

When respected school leaders collaborate, they build a sense of ownership and commitment to the desired change. Making positive changes to culture and climate requires time and intentional effort. All school leaders need to be persistent and consistent in promoting positive behaviors and addressing challenges as they arise. School leaders must seek regular feedback from all stakeholders about their experiences and perceptions of their school culture. They should use this feedback to adjust and make improvements as needed. When school leaders are flexible, open to change, and able to handle constructive criticism, they can improve their school's culture and climate.

Positive school culture and climate are essential for creating an environment where students can thrive academically, socially, and emotionally. A positive school culture can contribute to a supportive school culture and climate. When a respected school leader fosters a sense of belonging, ensures safety and well-being, promotes respectful relationships, and maintains high expectations, schools are supportive and can create a caring, effective, and respectful learning community for all stakeholders.

The following case study provides an example of one principal's experience of changing the school culture and climate from negative to positive. Here are some steps and ideas for getting started and/or facilitating a positive school culture and climate in your school.

Case Study: Changing School Culture and Climate

For years, I heard the same complaints about the culture and climate of my high-achieving high school. These negative comments from the teachers and staff all came down to the fact that everyone had too much on their plate. They were being asked to take on more and more responsibilities in their classrooms (larger class sizes, diverse learning needs, students' social-emotional learning needs, new curriculum, etc.) with fewer schoolwide resources and funding and nothing being taken off their plates. There was also a high turnover in administration, which caused teachers and staff to feel anxious and stressed at work. All the complaints from teachers and staff were valid and were contributors to the negative school culture.

Research shows that the culture and climate of a school are linked to adults in the school. So, when adults in a school experience a poor climate and culture, it directly affects student performance (Pechtold, 2018). According to Gray et al. (2017), "Positive school climate also has the potential to contribute to teacher mental health and to provide an optimal environment to support student learning and growth" (p. 203). This is a respected school leader's ultimate goal: to create a positive school culture and climate.

The principal of the school was ultimately responsible for creating and ensuring a positive school culture and climate. It was up to me as part of the leadership team to develop and implement a plan for change because the school had a negative culture and climate. My leadership team (assistant principal, dean, curriculum director, and department chair) wasted no time in creating a plan that included several steps to create a positive culture and climate in our school.

My first step was to sit down and meet with every adult in the building. These meetings were 20 minutes in length and optional (over summer break). The goal of these meetings was to collect qualitative data from all the adults in the school. First, collect data on the adults' perception of the school culture and climate. Solicit ideas about ways to improve the culture and climate of the school. Create a "collective responsibility" culture and climate in the school by encouraging and empowering adult leaders.

The second step was to meet with the students. I met with students individually and in small groups. Throughout the year, I attended student club meetings (academic, athletic, leadership, etc.). These groups of students could range anywhere from two or three students to 15 to 20 students in attendance. If groups of students wanted to meet with the leadership team, we made the time.

The final step was meeting with the parents. I held "Coffee With the Principal" sessions two to three times per month throughout the year. I attended parent meetings throughout the year. I met with groups and individual parents when requested and sought out groups that I believed would give me real feedback and solutions for changing our school culture.

The leadership's goal was to go on a "listening tour" and genuinely listen to the teachers, staff, students, parents, and community members. Our goal as a leadership team was to exemplify the core values in every meeting, action, and decision we made that year. According to Arencibia (2023), "Leading by example isn't merely a catchphrase; it is the backbone of culture transformation." Our leadership team understood the goal and how incredibly important it was to be united and consistent in our interactions with all stakeholders.

Change was slow to start and it took some time before we began to notice positive changes in our school. In collaboration with the faculty, the leadership team created a program that addressed bullying and harassment and a program that educated all stakeholders on the importance of diversity, equity, and inclusion. Students were asked through anonymous surveys and brown bag lunch meetings what changes could be implemented to improve the school's culture and climate. School leaders and faculty observed students' behavior in the hallways, cafeteria, and classrooms to gauge the overall mood of the students. Each faculty meeting began with "Shout-out celebrations" recognizing faculty and staff members who contributed to creating a positive school culture and climate. School monthly assemblies began with faculty members recognizing students who went above and beyond to create a positive school culture and climate.

However, in the end, everyone took ownership of creating a positive school culture and climate. We still have a long way to go and a lot of work to do, but we have started to create a culture and climate where everyone in the school feels safe to have a voice and where everyone takes ownership of creating a positive school culture and climate.

Reflection Questions:

Q1 If surveyed, what do you think your students, faculty, parents, and school community members would say about the culture and climate in your school?

Q2 How do you, as a respected school leader, create a positive school culture and climate?

References

Arencibia, D. (2023). Building a positive school culture: Seven steps for success. *Principal Leadership*, *24*(4).

Cakiroglu, O., Akkan, Y., & Guven, B. (2012). Analyzing the effect of web-based instruction applications to school culture within technology integration. *Educational Sciences: Theory and Practice*, *12*(2), 1043–1048.

Deal, T. E., & Peterson, K. D. (1999). *Shaping school culture: The heart of leadership*. Jossey-Bass.

Fullan, M. (2002). The change leader. *Educational Leadership*, *59*(8), 16–20.

Fullan, M. (2008). *The six secrets of change. What the leaders do to help their organization survive and thrive*. Jossey-Bass.

Gordana, S. (2020, July 30). *The ultimate guide to shaping school culture*. Unify High School. https://unifyhighschool.org/shaping-school-culture/

Gray, C., Wilcox, G., & Nordstokke, D. (2017). Teacher mental health, school climate, inclusive education, and student learning: A review. *Canadian Psychology/psychologie canadienne*, *58*(3), 203–210. https://doi.org/10.1037/cap0000117

GreatSchools. (2020, July 20). *The power of positive school culture* [Video]. YouTube. https://www.youtube.com/watch?v=zb3JRvOoMGs

Gruenert, S., & Whitaker, T. (2015). *School culture rewired: How to define, assess, and transform it*. Association for Supervision and Curriculum Development.

Habegger, S. (2008). The principal's role in successful schools: Creating a positive school culture. *Principal, 88*(1), 42–46.

International Baccalaureate. (n.d.). *About*. Retrieved July 22, 2024, from https://www.ibo.org/about-the-ib/

Kane, L., Hoff, N., Cathcart, A., Heifner, A., Palmon, S., & Peterson, R. L. (2016, February). *School climate and culture. Strategy brief.* University of Nebraska, Lincoln and the Nebraska Department of Education. https://k12engagement.unl.edu/school-climate-and-culture/

Maxwell, J. C. (2022). *The 21 irrefutable laws of leadership*. Thomas Nelson.

National School Climate Center. (2007). *The school climate challenge: Narrowing the gap between school climate research and school climate policy, practice guidelines and teacher education policy*. https://schoolclimate.org/wp-content/uploads/2021/05/school-climate-challenge-web.pdf

Pechtold, K. (2018). Changing school culture: A case study. *Principal Leadership, 18*(5), 44–47.

Schein, E. H. (2010). *Organizational culture and leadership* (4th ed.). Wiley.

Starkey, J. (2023). Effective strategies for building and sustaining a positive school culture and climate. *Academy of Educational Leadership Journal, 27*(S2), 1–3.

5
Supporting a School's Well-Being

School leaders are familiar with the growing focus on well-being in schools. The postpandemic increase in mental health needs for students and faculty members has become urgent. According to Rebora (2022), many educators believe we can no longer offer programs or initiatives that are "one-and-done" and do not work for our schools. He stated, "Well-being must become an integral part of what schools do." When school leaders take the time and effort to invest in the well-being of their schools, it improves academic outcomes; supports mental, physical, and emotional health; fosters a positive and inclusive school culture; and reinforces the long-term success and resilience of students, staff, and the wider school community. Miles et al. (2022) remind us of what Henry David Thoreau once said: "How we spend our time is a function of our values – and how time is allocated during the school day reflects what is important to the community, intentionally or unintentionally." Respected school leaders prioritize the well-being of their stakeholders because they realize in doing so, they are ultimately investing in the holistic development and future success of their entire school community. As John Maxwell (2011) stated, "When people feel liked, cared for, included, valued, and trusted, they begin to work together with their leader and each other."

A school's well-being is a multifaceted concept encompassing the emotional, social, academic, and physical aspects of students, faculty, staff, and community experiences and development.

Well-being can be defined as a core value in a school's mission and strategic planning, ensuring that it is embedded in all aspects of school life. It is paramount for the school leader to establish a clear vision for the well-being of the school. This vision needs to ensure that the school's well-being is a priority. It is also critical for the school leader to communicate this priority to the students, faculty, and school community because the well-being of the school directly affects the overall success and health of the entire community. When the well-being of a school is the focus, it is possible to create a positive and nurturing environment that fosters learning and personal growth.

Why should school leaders prioritize well-being in schools? The well-being in schools is crucial because it supports all stakeholders in making healthy lifestyle choices and helps them to understand its impact on personal health. According to Buecker et al. (2018), well-being supports intrinsic motivation, decreases disciplinary problems, increases academic achievement, improves school satisfaction, and leads to the flourishing of individuals and communities. It also helps develop important traits such as flexibility, open-mindedness, and tolerance that can help students, faculty, and staff adapt to change, accept others, and consider different perspectives. In other words, if students, faculty, and staff feel better about their experience in school they will do better.

How does a school leader begin to prioritize their school's well-being? It begins with emphasizing the importance of well-being to students, faculty, and parents through consistent communication, policies, and everyday actions. Many of John's school parents know that he cares deeply about the well-being of their community. If a respected school leader is going to be a champion for well-being in their school community, then they need to be an excellent communicator of that message. John's community identifies him as an excellent communicator. One parent stated, "I found my principal to be very hands-on with his students and appreciate his dedication and communication." Another parent referred to John as a great communicator. According to several parents in his community, he is consistent when it comes to his weekly outreach to families. As a respected school leader, when you receive positive comments about your communication from parents, like the ones cited here, it creates an environment where everyone in the community feels valued and respected.

To prioritize a school's well-being, a respected school leader models positive leadership attributes such as leading by example and being empathic and approachable. One of John's students commented, "My principal's empathy shows through everyday conversations and meetings I've had with him." Another student stated, "He is amazing and approachable." Respected school leaders demonstrate positive well-being attributes and create a supportive environment that helps students thrive both academically and personally.

There is a growing concern among school leaders about creating a safe environment in their schools. It's important for respected school leaders to build a safe school environment where everyone in the school feels like they have support and the skills to ask for the help that they need.

School safety is at the forefront of most school leaders' minds. When students and staff walk into their classrooms each morning, family members and school leaders should feel safe and happy that the children are learning and the faculty and staff are enjoying their jobs. Instead, many leaders are fearful and anxious because of ongoing school violence. When we think about school safety, we cannot help but think about the school shootings that have occurred across the United States over the past several years. Education Week (2024) reported 26 school shootings that resulted in injuries or deaths in 2024 and 38 in 2023. For school leaders, who are entrusted with the safety of students, faculty, and staff, these tragedies underscore the urgent need to reinforce and rethink our schools' safety plans. It is essential that all students be able to attend schools that provide a safe environment where they can learn and fully engage in their studies without distraction and worry about physical safety concerns.

A respected school leader is ultimately responsible for having a comprehensive safety plan. The safety plan should be detailed and address various potential threats and emergencies. The aim of this plan is to protect students from bullying, exposure to weapons, the sale and use of drugs, harassment, and violence. It is a plan to keep our students, faculty, and staff safe at school.

The school leader will need to establish a safety and threat assessment team. This team should include key personnel like the principal, assistant principal, teachers, mental health professionals, and safety officers. One of the goals of this safety and threat assessment team is to outline clear procedures for crisis prevention, preparedness, response, and recovery. The safety plan should be reviewed, revised, and practiced through drills and simulations throughout the school year. According to the Centers for Disease Control's (n.d.) Youth Violence Prevention resources, "About one in five High School students report being bullied on school property in the past year." In a report by the Institute of Education Sciences (2022), 70 percent of public schools report an increase in the percentage of their students seeking mental health services at school since the start of the COVID-19 pandemic, and 76 percent of public schools cite an increase in staff voicing concerns about their students exhibiting symptoms such as depression, anxiety, and trauma. It is imperative that school leaders create a safe and nurturing environment that fosters learning and personal growth in their school communities. One student at Elena's school commented, "My principal is always making sure we are safe every day." As a principal, this is what you want to hear from all your students.

Although we can never completely guarantee the safety of our students, faculty, and staff, respected school leaders do everything in their power to protect them. Roberts et al. (2023) reported that superintendents from across the United States gathered in 2021 at the Institute for Educator Innovation summit. The goal of this summit was to create new strategies to defend students' physical, mental, and emotional health. These educational leaders agreed on five key factors with a holistic approach to school security and gave actionable next steps for district leaders. These are: 1) upgrade school facilities as a start, not a solution; 2) strengthen school–student relationships as a critical line of defense; 3) revisit threat-training policies, protocols, and procedures; 4) elevate community engagement to ensure everyone plays a role; and 5) improve trust between school resource officers and students to build a safer school. For students to learn, they need to feel safe. Respected school leaders invest in the physical, social, and emotional safety of their students, faculty, and staff.

Why is nurturing mental health and social-emotional well-being in schools so important? For school leaders, mental health has become an increasing concern. According to a panel discussion in *Principal Leadership* (Charboneau-Folch et al., 2022), it is important to nurture the mental health of students because it promotes success in their future. Students can obtain the tools they need to be able to communicate openly and effectively about how they are coping with their mental health. It also allows them to ask for help and not be ashamed about it. Schools are trying to have a holistic student approach, and a major part of their academic success is their social-emotional well-being. If we do not address our students' mental health issues, it will be a great challenge to educate them.

Respected school leaders help support the mental health and well-being of their students when they ensure students' basic needs are met, implement restorative justice practices, use a student-centered approach to behavior, and establish strong relationships with their students. When students feel safe and connected to the adults in their school, trust is built. Building trusting relationships is key to being a respected school leader. Vanessa was asked about how she promotes the social-emotional and mental health and well-being of her students and faculty in her school. She stated, "I focus on this FIRST. We can't work on educational areas unless we work on the social-emotional and the mental health issues of our students and faculty." She created areas in her school to help the faculty with their mental health such as a massage area with chairs and aromatherapy for the faculty to use when they are feeling stressed or overwhelmed. She claims it's all about paying attention to the needs of the people in your building.

Respected school leaders prioritize mental health and well-being in their schools. The New Jersey School Boards Association (2023) reported on a CDC action guide for student mental health and well-being:

> Schools can help promote the mental health and well-being of students through education, prevention, and early intervention efforts. They provide an opportunity to reach a large number of youths with strategies that can lessen the impact of negative experience and improve students' health and well-being.

The CDC action guide is meant to help school leaders build on what they are already doing in their schools to promote students' mental health. The goal of the CDC action guide is to provide school leaders with strategies, approaches, and practices that can improve students' mental health. The CDC (2023) states:

> School leaders create a nurturing and inclusive environment that fosters positive mental health and well-being for all stakeholders. This involves developing policies and procedures that prioritize mental health and well-being, establishing a culture of understanding and empathy, and promoting open communication within the school community.

Promoting mental health and well-being in schools is not only a moral obligation but also the right thing to do. Respected school leaders set the tone for creating a supportive and nurturing environment that promotes the mental health and well-being of the whole school community.

Students spend a significant amount of time at school, which has led to the school environment being a major focus of mental health research (Hogberg et al., 2020; Kidger et al., 2012). Bullying and harassment adversely impact the school environment and the school's well-being. Bullying has wide-ranging and potentially severe impacts on students' mental health, well-being, and academic performance (Yassin, 2024). It can affect students' emotional well-being, behavior, academic performance, and long-term mental health outcomes. Effective antibullying and harassment policies and interventions are crucial for protecting students' mental health. Respected school leaders create effective policies for bullying and harassment that include managing peer pressure in their schools. They promote an atmosphere of acceptance and inclusion to ensure that students feel safe and supported in the school community.

How does bullying affect student well-being? It is important to define bullying and what is involved. Olweus (2013) states bullying involves repeated hurtful actions between peers where an imbalance of power exists. According to a McLean Hospital (2025) web page:

> Bullying happens between someone who has more power and is more aggressive than their targeted person. A bully uses that power, whether it's physical strength, being more popular, or knowing embarrassing information to hurt or control the person they're bullying.

Research shows that bullying comes in many forms and can happen anytime. The most common forms of bullying are: 1) physical bullying: hitting, striking, kicking, shoving, intentional tripping, or spitting on someone; 2) verbal bullying: teasing, threats of physical harm, name-calling, using offensive language, yelling, or harassment; and 3) cyberbullying, which takes place in the digital world on cell phones, tablets, and computers. According to the McLean Hospital page, "Cyberbullying is a significant concern. It can have a major impact on a young person's mental health. Adolescents who are the victims of cyberbullying are more likely to experience depression, anxiety, and academic difficulties."

Bullying and harassment can have severe negative effects on students' mental health. Students who are bullied are more likely to develop depression. The most common signs of depression include sleep problems, appetite changes, emotional disturbances, and even thoughts of suicide. Arseneault et al.'s (2010) review of the mental health consequences of bullying and harassment for children found that bullying and harassment are associated with severe symptoms of mental health problems including self-harm and suicidality. According to the World Health Organization (2014), suicide is a major concern in the United States and globally. The CDC (2023) reported a total of 48,183 persons (of all ages) died from suicide in 2021. Across the United States, suicide was the 11th leading cause of death overall, accounting for approximately 1.4% of all deaths. The CDC reported that in 2021, there were 1,952 suicides among U.S. youths ages 14-18, making suicide the third leading cause of death for this age group and accounting for approximately one-fifth of deaths (18.6 percent) among this age group (Verlenden et al., 2024). There is a concerning pattern of increased suicide risk during the school year, and respected school leaders are increasingly recognizing the need to include suicide prevention efforts in their schools' mental health plans.

Students may also develop anxiety because they fear bullying and harassment at every turn (Yassin, 2024). Bullying and harassment interfere with students' ability to learn and succeed academically. Students who are regularly bullied and harassed may not want to attend school or participate in school-related activities. When students miss school, it is harder for them to keep up with their studies, and academic performance often suffers. Students may feel a loss of self-confidence if they are bullied and harassed. As an example, this may lead to students feeling they are not as good at a particular sport as the person bullying and harassing them. This in turn may prevent them from trying out for a team because they are experiencing self-criticism and are often harsh on themselves. When students are bullied and harassed, they often feel so bad about themselves that they isolate from their peers, family members, and friends.

Bullying and harassment are universal issues that can have detrimental mental health effects on the individuals involved. However, schools can prevent or reduce incidents by developing students' social and emotional skills (National Education Association, 2021). When respected school leaders address the social and emotional needs of both victims and perpetrators, social-emotional learning (SEL) can help break the cycle of bullying and harassment.

How can SEL programs help break the cycle of bullying and harassment? A significant meta-analysis of school-based universal interventions showed that implementing high-quality SEL programs in schools can significantly increase students' academic and behavioral outcomes (Durlak et al., 2011). As a result of this study and many others like it, schools began to adopt SEL curricula and programs to strengthen students' social and emotional skills (Boston Consulting Group, 2018; Domitrovich et al., 2017). Haynes (2021) suggests school leaders should be encouraged to expand and strengthen their efforts to implement SEL. SEL programs focus on developing essential skills such as empathy, emotion management, and social problem-solving, which can foster a safe and inclusive school environment. In a ten-year study of elementary and middle school principals conducted by the National Association of Elementary School Principals, Fuller et al. (2018) concluded that SEL was the top issue of concern for elementary principals. In Elena's school, they believe that SEL is as important as academics. She believes that self-regulation and structure are really important. Her school has implemented morning meetings in the daily schedule as the "bedrock" of the school.

Districts across the country are prioritizing instructional practices like SEL because the well-being of administrators, teachers, and students has become the focus. According to the NEA (2021), SEL is the foundation of academic success, and addressing mental health issues must be a priority in our school communities: "Supporting our students' and educators' mental health with SEL helps the whole school community thrive" (NEA, 2021). A survey called "State of Education," conducted by Teachers Pay Teachers (2022), declared, "Our school leaders have provided us with more funding for interventionists, a school counselor, and more resources for differentiation in the classroom." Luis's school has a full-time social worker and counselor on staff to support students' mental health. In the classroom, teachers have established a "calming place" for students to use because of the violence some students experience at home. Luis also conducts a needs assessment twice a year (fall and January) to collect ideas about what the school can do to help support mental health and SEL.

As educators, we know how difficult it is for teachers to support students' social-emotional needs when their own well-being is suffering. As a respected school leader, Luis considers the well-being of his faculty. With respect to his teachers, Luis states: "Because of the job we have, we need an outlet." He makes it a priority to support them as they focus on their well-being and asks each faculty member, "What are you doing for YOU?" His goal for supporting the well-being of the faculty is for each faculty member to identify one thing they would like to do for themselves. Darling-Hammond et al. (2020) state: "Recent data indicated that young people are experiencing chronic stress and trauma as they navigate basic needs and health concerns, a lack of connectivity to their school communities, and exhaustion from constant anxiety about the future." They indicate that SEL skills, mental health supports, and restorative practices are critical for supporting students after the pandemic. Students face many challenges, uncertainty, and stress during this time. "Infusing SEL through both virtual and in-person instruction will help to mitigate the pandemic's impact on lifelong success and learning" (p. 33).

Respected school leaders play a pivotal role in creating a positive school environment, and SEL is a critical part of those efforts. The most widely known and used SEL framework comes from Collaborative for Academic, Social, and Emotional Learning (CASEL). Developed in 1994, CASEL's goal is to deliver high-quality SEL from Pre-K through high school. The CASEL framework competencies and skills include:

- Self-awareness, including skills such as identifying emotions, developing an accurate self-perception, recognizing strengths, and developing self-confidence and self-efficacy
- Self-management, including skills such as impulse control, stress management, self-discipline, self-motivation, goal-setting, and organizational skills
- Social awareness, including skills such as perspective-taking, empathy, appreciating diversity, and respect for others
- Relationship skills, including skills such as communication, social engagement, and relationship-building teamwork

- Responsible decision-making, including skills such as identifying problems, analyzing situations, solving problems, evaluating, reflecting, and developing ethical responsibility

CASEL (2017) defines SEL as "how children and adults learn to understand and manage emotions, set goals, show empathy for others, establish positive relationships, and make responsible decisions." Effective SEL programs help students develop and learn the skills they need to accomplish CASEL's definition of SEL (CASEL, 2017; Lemerise & Arsenio, 2000). However, increasing demands on teachers means they need more support from their school administrators in bringing SEL programs to the classroom. The "State of Education" survey conducted by Teachers Pay Teachers (2022) found that "64% of the teachers stated their students' social-emotional needs were too much to handle on their own, and 90% of teachers said their concern for students' mental health and social-emotional needs has increased compared to before the pandemic" (p. 5).

Respected school leaders prioritize time for in-depth professional development sessions about SEL, an opportunity to practice SEL, and provide ongoing support for teachers with this work (Teachers Pay Teachers, 2022). Teachers need to build the skills necessary to deliver SEL with confidence. At John's high school, the first few weeks of each semester are devoted to SEL. Lessons are developed and discussed with faculty before implementation, and a concerted effort is made to help students feel their school is home. They also use their school's "Multi-Tiered System of Support" (MTSS). This approach allows the school to provide increasingly intensive support only to those students who need them, based on ongoing assessment and data analysis. The students are divided into three groups: 1) Universal Screening: all students are screened at regular intervals (e.g., beginning and middle of the year) in academic, behavioural, social-emotional, and attendance domains to identify those at risk for poor outcomes; 2) Data-Based Decision Making: school teams review screening and progress monitoring data to determine which students require additional support and at what tier; and 3) Flexible Grouping: students can move between tiers based on their response to interventions, ensuring that support is responsive and not static.

To achieve the full potential of SEL, school leaders must integrate SEL into all aspects of the school and programs. This includes what happens in the lunchroom, playground, hallways, and during extracurricular activities (Mahoney et al., 2018; National Commission on Social, Emotional, and Academic Development, 2019). Many of Elena's students commented on how she is fair, kind, polite, and caring, and believes in the school and her students. One student stated: "My principal always says hi to me in the hallway and lunchroom, and sometimes she goes to my classroom."

How do school leaders integrate SEL? According to the Search Institute (2020),

> It lies in relationships. Relationships are a critically important mechanism by which youth learn about themselves and about how to communicate and connect with another person. And, when these relationships develop in a context that supports and celebrates diversity, equity, and inclusion (DEI), they have the potential to be truly transformative.
>
> (p. 3)

SEL and DEI are interconnected approaches that can work together to support student well-being in schools.

It is important for students to have strong relationships at school and in their communities to support their well-being and reach their educational goals. However, the process of building those relationships is not the same for everyone. A respected school leader is aware of the challenges students and staff encounter at their school and advocates for them. One of Luis's faculty stated: "My principal is an advocate for brown and black students. The principal is unafraid to defend and represent the students and staff in front of the higher school officials." A community member at Luis's school commented:

> I appreciate our principal's advocacy for his students and staff. The principal is not afraid to [address the] issues.

This year we received a high number of refugee students and the principal has embraced the students and families with open arms and has worked on making them feel welcomed in our school community.

School leaders' responsibilities go beyond managing administrative tasks in today's rapidly changing educational landscape. School leaders are expected to foster an environment where every student feels valued and supported regardless of background. When John was asked how he creates an inclusive and equitable learning environment for his students, he stated, "Today, our students can be found in our hallways and on our playing fields from 6:30 am until 7:30 pm." A teacher from another school responded when John asked her if she knew about his school saying, "Yeah, that's the school where none of the kids want to go home."

Diversio (n.d.), creators of an analytic platform that tracks DEI for organizations, states:

> DEI in education is shaping the next generation of thinkers, leaders, and global citizens. Barriers like systemic racism and poverty can limit students' access to equal education. When educational institutions prioritize DEI, they should make strategic, data-informed decisions to shape their initiatives. Integrating DEI into education brings valuable benefits to students and educators.

The American Psychological Association (APA, 2021) states that DEI "is a conceptual framework that promotes the fair treatment and full participation of all people, especially populations that have historically been underrepresented or subject to discrimination because of their background, identity, disability, etc." Adapted from the APA's equity, diversity, and inclusion framework, here is a breakdown of each term:

- ♦ Diversity – A measure of the representation of different groups in a community or organization, including their identity, background, culture, and experiences.
- ♦ Equity – The practice of distributing resources based on need, rather than offering the same opportunity to

everyone regardless of circumstance. Equity acknowledges that people don't start at the same level and aims to correct imbalances.

◆ Inclusion – The creation of an environment where everyone feels welcome, valued, and respected, and is able to fully participate. Inclusion involves welcoming differences, listening to different perspectives, and ensuring that everyone feels a sense of belonging.

When addressing DEI comprehensively, a respected school leader can create an environment where all students and staff feel respected, valued, and empowered to succeed. One of Elena's faculty members commented: "My principal is a risk-taking leader who often takes chances on her teachers." There are many ways respected school leaders address DEI in their schools. They create an inclusive school culture. This involves modeling empathy, respect, and collaboration and encouraging open dialogue about diversity and inclusion. One of Elena's faculty members stated: "Throughout the year of teaching, I have felt safe, supported, driven, and inspired as an innovative leader." Respected school leaders celebrate different cultures and backgrounds through school curricula and events. When Elena was asked how she created a more inclusive and equitable learning environment for her students, she commented:

> We have a mariachi band, NOT a choir. I saw this as an opportunity to educate others. We serve students that are differently abled. It's hard work and we don't shy away from it at our school. We are proud of the work we do as a school. Everyone is part of the mariachi music program and they perform at community events. This is a huge investment of money – all the students have mariachi attire. The mariachi program needs to live beyond me. My hope is that my legacy is what I did is what students needed. I am here to make the change that everybody aligns to our mission, vision, and values that we developed over time.

A respected school leader develops and enforces policies that promote inclusivity and address systemic barriers. This includes creating antidiscrimination policies, implementing inclusive curriculum standards, and allocating resources equitably to ensure all students have access to necessary support. Elena commented:

> I am adamant about cultural and linguistical diversity and it's very difficult to do. I serve in a dual-language school where the dominant language of instruction is Spanish in our dual-language classrooms. Everything we do must be in two languages [English and Spanish]. Programs and after-school programs are in English and Spanish.

Investing in ongoing professional development for staff is crucial. This includes cultural competency training, workshops on effective teaching strategies for diverse learners, and raising awareness about unconscious biases. Respected school leaders involve students, parents, and community members in decision-making processes to ensure all voices are heard. One of Elena's students commented: "Our principal is always checking on us. The other day she came to my lunch table and asked about our opinion on the lunches. I was completely honest with her and she understood. I was happy because she actually listened to me." Respected school leaders can involve stakeholders by having regular town hall meetings, forming parent-teacher associations, and creating community partnerships.

By implementing these strategies, the respected school leader can effectively address the mental health of their students and faculty and implement effective SEL and DEI programs in their schools. A safe environment that honors the mental health of all stakeholders can yield a place for the respected school leader to thrive.

The following case study provides an example of Elena's experience of prioritizing well-being in her school.

Case Study: How Is Your School's Well-Being?

"Start where you are. Use what you have. Do what you can." Our assistant principal would utter these words at the beginning of our Wellness Wednesday building meeting. In the years after the COVID pandemic, we recognized the need to rebuild our school culture and focus on caring for ourselves to serve our students and school community. We made wellness as crucial as academics in our recovery back to high achievement by connecting at least once a month, engaging in mindfulness exercises, and having fun together as a staff. We practiced wellness intentionally; the mindfulness techniques selected were transferable to our classrooms, and we encouraged our staff to implement these strategies with our students during their SEL time at the beginning of each school day. We placed so much value and emphasis on taking care of ourselves that it translated into taking care of each other, and the human connection in our school strengthened beyond expectation. The impact of these practices was felt throughout our community, and our students' academic achievement skyrocketed, taking our school to new heights. When you care for yourself and each other, you are a more intentional teacher who can better care of your students. As flight attendants instruct us, when your emergency oxygen mask deploys, put yours on before you assist others. Two years after the pandemic, our school was recognized by the Illinois State Board of Education as an exemplary school due to the high increase in student achievement in one academic year. We have always called ourselves a "family," and the strong bonds we forged by prioritizing wellness solidified our commitment to relationships at our school, translating into innumerable benefits throughout the school and community.

Reflection Questions:

Q1 What practices are you currently focused on that improve wellness in your school?

Q2 How would you determine additional wellness practices to add to your existing repertoire?

References

American Psychological Association. (2021). *Inclusive language guide.* https://www.apa.org/about/apa/equity-diversity-inclusion/language-guidelines

Arseneault, L., Bowes, L., & Shakoor, S. (2010). Bullying victimization in youths and mental health problems: "Much ado about nothing"? *Psychology Medicine, 40*(5), 717–729. https://doi.org/10.1017/S0033291709991383

Boston Consulting Group. (2018). *Social, emotional, and academic development field landscape analysis.* https://www.aspeninstitute.org/wp-content/uploads/2018/09/NC-SEAD-Field-Landscape-AnalysisvF_092118.pdf

Buecker, S., Nuraydin, S., Simonsmeier, B., Schneider, M., & Luhmann, M. (2018). Subjective well-being and academic achievement: A meta-analysis. *Journal of Research in Personality, 74,* 83–94. https://doi.org/10.1016/j.jrp.2018.02.007

Centers for Disease Control and Prevention. (2023). *Promoting mental health and well-being in schools: An action guide for school and district leaders.* https://stacks.cdc.gov/view/cdc/136371

Centers for Disease Control and Prevention. (n.d.). *About violence prevention.* Retrieved October 1, 2024, from https://www.cdc.gov/violence-prevention/about/index.html

Charboneau-Folch, A., Frieson, L., & Petersen, K. (2022). *Roundtable: Students' mental health* [Principal leadership article]. National Association of Secondary School Principals. https://www.nassp.org/publication/principal-leadership/volume-22-2021-2022/principal-leadership-april-2022/roundtable-students-mental-health/

Collaborative for Academic Social and Emotional Learning. (2017). *What is SEL?* https://drc.casel.org/what-is-sel/

Darling-Hammond, L., Schachner, A., & Edgerton, A. K. (2020). *Restarting and reinventing school: Learning in the time of COVID and beyond*. Learning Policy Institute. https://learningpolicyinstitute.org/sites/default/files/product-files/Restart_Reinvent_Schools_COVID_Priority2_Distance_Learning.pdf

Diversio. (n.d.). *DEI in education*. Retrieved September 6, 2024, from https://diversio.com/industries/dei-education/

Domitrovich, C. E., Durlak, J. A., Staley, K. C., & Weissberg, R. P. (2017). Social-emotional competence: An essential factor for promoting positive adjustment and reducing risk in school children. *Child Development*, 8(2), 408–416. https://doi.org/10.1111/cdev.12739

Durlak, J. A., Weissberg, R. P., Dymnicki, A. B., Taylor, R. D., & Schellinger, K. B. (2011). The impact of enhancing students' social and emotional learning: A meta-analysis of school-based universal interventions. *Child Development*, 82(1), 405–432. https://doi.org/10.1111/j.1467-8624.2010.01564.x

Education Week. (2024, September 6). *School shootings this year: How many and where. Education Week's 2024 school shooting tracker*. https://www.edweek.org/leadership/school-shootings-this-year-how-many-and-where/2024/01

Fuller, E. J., Young, M. D., Richardson, M. S., Pendola, A., & Winn, K. M. (2018). *The pre-K-8 school leader in 2018: A 10-year study*. National Association of Elementary School Principals. https://www.naesp.org/sites/default/files/NAESP%2010-YEAR%20REPORT_2018.pdf

Haynes, N. M. (2021). The critical role of school leaders in implementing social and emotional learning. *Ed*, 2. https://www.globalcitizenshipfoundation.org/issue/02

Hogberg, B., Strandh, M., & Hagquist, C. (2020). Gender and secular trends in adolescent mental health over 24 years – the role of school-related stress. *Social Science and Medicine*, 250. https://doi.org/10.1016/j.socscimed.2020.112890

Institute of Education Sciences. (2022). *How to create a safe learning environment: 6 examples*. National Center for Education Statistics. https://nces.ed.gov/fastfacts/display.asp?id=1130

Kidger, J., Araya, R., Donovan, J., & Gunnell, D. (2012). The effect of the school environment on the emotional health of adolescents:

A systematic review. *Pediatrics, 129*(5), 925–949. https://doi.org/10.1542/peds.2011-2248

Lemerise, E. A., & Srsenio, W. F. (2000). An integrated model of emotion processes and cognition in social information processing. *Child Development, 71*(1), 107–118. https://doi.org/10.1111/1467-8624.00124

Mahoney, J. L., Durlak, J. A., & Weissberg, R. P. (2018). An update on social and emotional learning outcome research. *Phi Delta Kappan, 100*(4), 18–23. https://doi.org/10.1177/0031721718815668

Maxwell, J. (2011, September 5). *Level 2 – permission: You can't lead people until you like people.* https://www.johnmaxwell.com/blog/level-2-permission-you-cant-lead-people-until-you-like-people/

McLean Hospital. (2025, May 5). *The mental health impact of bullying on kids and teens.* https://www.mcleanhospital.org/essential/bullying-kids-teens

Miles, S., Pope, D., Villeneuve, J. C., & Selby, S. T. (2022). Making time for well-being. *Educational Leadership, 79*(9), 60–65.

National Commission on Social, Emotional, and Academic Development. (2019). *From a nation at risk to a nation at hope.* Aspen Institute.

National Education Association. (2021, August). *Resources on social emotional learning (SEL) and student and educator mental health.* https://www.nea.org/professional-excellence/student-engagement/tools-tips/resources-social-emotional-learning-sel-and-student-and-educator-mental-health

New Jersey School Boards Association. (2023, December 11). *CDC publishes action guide on promoting mental health and well-being in schools.* https://www.njsba.org/school-board-notes/cdc-publishes-action-guide-on-promoting-mental-health-and-well-being-in-schools/

Olweus, D. (2013). School bullying: Development and some important challenges. *Annual Review of Clinical Psychology, 9,* 751–780. https://doi.org/10.1146/annurev-clinpsy-050212-185516

Rebora, A. (2022). Beyond lip service on school well-being. *Educational Leadership, 79*(9).

Roberts, D., Levett, A., & Downs, S. (2023, June 1). Five critical strategies to make your school safer. *Education Week.* https://www.edweek.org/leadership/opinion-5-critical-strategies-to-make-your-school-safer/2023/06

Search Institute. (2020). *The intersection of developmental relationships, equitable environments, and SEL*. Search Institute.

Teachers Pay Teachers. (2022). *State of education: National survey findings shed light on teachers' concerns and the support they need.* https://ecdn.teacherspayteachers.com/static/state_of_education_report_by_tpt_feb2022.pdf

Verlenden, J. V., Fodeman, A., Wilkins, N., Jones, S. E., Moore, S., Cornett, K., Sims, V., Saelee, R., & Brener, N. D. (2024, October 10). Mental health and suicide risk among high school students and protective factors – youth risk behavior survey, United States, 2023. *Morbidity and Mortality Weekly Report Supplements, 73*(4), 79–86. https://doi.org/10.15585/mmwr.su7304a9

World Health Organization. (2014). *Preventing suicide: A global imperative.* who.int/iris/bitstream/handle/10665/131056/9789241564779_eng.pdf

Yassin, F. (2024, March 29). *Bullying in school and young people's mental health*. The Wave Clinic. https://thewaveclinic.com/blog/bullying-in-school-and-young-peoples-mental-health/

6

School Leader Challenges

"It's Vanessa. Sorry I didn't pick up right away and it took me a while to get back to you. We just had a shooting outside my school." Those were the first words from our respected school leader when she returned my call. I just sat there, concerned and nervous, and said when we chatted later that day, "Well, Vanessa, it doesn't get too much more difficult than that. Hope you and your students are OK." The good news was, at least in this case, they were.

All those who work in schools today are faced with myriad daunting challenges that can overwhelm them in their everyday work. This is especially true for the school leader as there are no easy days. At the top of any respected school leader's daily to-do list is doing the best for students – perhaps starting the day by saying good morning to as many as possible. But many things can and do get in the way of a simple morning greeting. This chapter discusses five significant challenges and reflects upon how school leaders deal with them. The respected school leader exemplars demonstrate how this type of school leader is supported, encouraged, assisted, and even a bit comforted when being respected. Respect may not carry the day, but it certainly goes a long way to make it more bearable.

This chapter originally planned to discuss nearly twenty challenges school leaders face. However, that large number was narrowed to five significant challenges, which demonstrate just how complex, difficult, and stressful school leaders' jobs have

DOI: 10.4324/9781003296201-6

become and how being respected can make a positive difference. As Malcom S. Forbes (n.d.) stated, "When things are bad, we take comfort in the thought that they could always get worse. And when they are, we find hope in the thought that things are so bad they have to get better."

School Safety, Security, and Emergency Preparedness

Vanessa's experience has become all too common for many schools in our country today. Many decades ago, many schools could have open access: doors and windows open, visitors came and went with ease, and students felt safe and free to learn and roam daily. Well, those days of open access are long gone. Abraham Maslow's (2013) hierarchy of needs has safety on the second tier of the pyramid. Only physiological needs (basic needs such as food and shelter) are more critical, and they are on tier one. School safety and security are paramount concerns requiring a school leader's immediate and sustained attention. Schools must be a place where students feel safe and secure so that learning can occur.

Cox et al. stated in a *Washington Post* article (2024), that there have been 413 school shootings in the United States since the Columbine shooting in 1999. The median age of a school shooter is 16, Black students are disproportionately affected by shootings, and more than 378,000 students have experienced gun violence since Columbine. The article stated, "Beyond the dead and wounded, children who witness the violence or cower behind locked doors to hide from it can be profoundly traumatized."

Lockdown and active shooter drills have been added to the list of drills, including annual fire and tornado drills. Safety is a constant concern and worry for any school leader, albeit heightened in many schools that are more prone to violence. In an attempt to make schools safer and use best practices, conducting security audits has become common for school leaders. School security has also become big business. Safety and security plans detail everything from active shooter drills to dealing with bomb threats and de-escalation techniques. Even deciding how to conduct active shooter drills is a challenge. Banerji and Mallon (2024) stated, "New York state, home to the largest school district in the country, is the latest to ban schools from conducting 'realistic' active shooter drills with fake blood and the sound of gunfire." No wonder a school leader's job has become such an immense challenge.

Natural disasters, such as tornadoes and hurricanes and sometimes fires, can create massive problems for school leaders, from closing schools for days to finding alternative schools for extended periods of time. Then there is simply dealing with inclement weather. One of our respected school leaders, Luis, keeps it simple when dealing with safety concerns that can affect learning. Luis said:

> When it comes to acts of God, we are ready and willing to do what is necessary to get my school up and running. For example, when it snows, I shovel and salt the grounds. When it rains, I put out mats. When it is hot and there is no AC, I buy portable ACs for classrooms. Being a respected leader is doing what is necessary for teaching and learning to occur.

And then there's the time Luis had to reschedule his appointment during the pandemic when I walked into his building. He said he was sorry and had to run to the Dollar Store because the school had just run out of disinfectant wipes. He leads by example and does what it takes to be safe, and he has earned the title of respected school leader for that.

Of course, there is a night and day difference between a school shooting and inclement weather. However, the respected school leader is called upon to do whatever is necessary to create the conditions, atmosphere, and environment needed for learning to occur. Simply put, learning is virtually impossible when one's mind is preoccupied with being safe.

Our respected school leader Elena, best summarized school safety and how a respected school leader is better equipped to manage safety daily. She said:

> School safety is top of mind for our district's leadership team. Being a respected school leader has helped me manage the challenge of being a welcoming school while also enforcing our safety policies and procedures. Communicating the rationale for these safety requirements and grounding them in what is in the best interest of our students, staff, and community has been a part of my success. Our community depends on my unwavering commitment to the safety of our school, and being a respected school leader has helped me achieve that goal.

School leaders are called upon to know how to respond to many challenging safety situations while creating a balance between a happy, healthy, open school and one that has a siege mentality. Think of it as a scale from 1 (all open access) to 10 (a complete lockdown atmosphere with outside security). School leaders are challenged to pick that number, create that balance, make the case for their choice, and know how to respond to whatever comes their way with their students' lives in the balance.

Schools must also be safe regarding health issues such as the pandemic and leaders must decide when and how to keep schools open or to reopen them. There is also the challenge of how to best manage chronic health conditions in the school community like diabetes and asthma, and even allergic reactions to peanuts or a head lice outbreak. You might be scratching your head here (no pun intended) and recalling those incidents you have managed and continue to manage today. Then there is knowing where a defibrillator is located and how to use it. These situations significantly affect the daily lives of everyone and weigh on the school leader, who needs to be knowledgeable about the seemingly endless list of guidelines and rules from the CDC, state public health agencies, state departments of education, the U.S. Department of Education, the American Academy of Pediatrics, local agencies, and their local school districts.

An example demonstrating the severity, complexity, and sensitivity of serious situations and how they can be successfully managed comes from Bultinck and Bush's (2009) *99 Ways to Lead and Succeed: Strategies and Stories for School Leaders*:

George Steffen, now the retired Superintendent of Trevor-Wilmot Consolidated School District in Wisconsin, suffered a major heart attack while at work, and his staff came to his rescue. They had been trained in the use of a defibrillator and CPR. As a result, they saved his life.

The Kenosha News in a front-page article quoted Pam Oldenburg, a Salem Fire and Rescue Department paramedic and an emergency medical services instructor: "If not for them we would have arrived and found a pulseless, not-breathing male on the ground. We would have found a dead body." This is a true story from the thousands that happen in our schools every day. The ones with positive endings engender heartfelt thanks. The ones that end in tragedy sadden us. Keeping school safe in all its facets and challenges is overwhelming. Being respected can be consoling, knowing one has done the best one could. We take the wins, regret the losses, pray, and move on to the next day.

Discipline

Discipline related to school safety and security is separated here for discussion because of its critical importance. A recent study, "Crime, Violence, Discipline, and Safety in U.S. Public Schools (National Center for Education Statistics, 2024), sheds light on this most extreme and disconcerting challenge. The survey's sampled findings include the following: 857,500 violent incidences in schools, 479,500 nonviolent incidences, 67 percent of schools reported at least one violent incident, 59 percent reported at least one physical attack or fight without a weapon, and 4 percent with a weapon. Law Insider (n.d.) says, *"Violent incident* means any act or attempted act of physical force that may cause, or has caused, physical injury to a person."

A school leader's day can become consumed with student discipline problems. Having great teachers significantly reduces the number of issues, as good teachers know how to look for problems before they even begin. Since colonial days, time and thought have gone into dealing with discipline. It's good we are no longer beating students with rods and using dunce caps! The best way to train new teachers and teach current ones how to manage a classroom is a work in progress. As has been said, the first place to start in having good classroom discipline is by having an excellent lesson plan.

The responsibility for maintaining disciplined schools resides with the local district and their school leaders knowing the rules, laws, regulations, and relevant court cases. There are many definitions of discipline, from simply maintaining a positive atmosphere for learning to the following from the National Center on Safe Supportive Learning Environments. (n.d.), "School discipline refers to the rules and strategies applied in school to manage student behavior and practices used to encourage self-discipline."

School leaders must manage an array of discipline matters each day. They address bullying and harassment (exponentially escalated by social media), general student disrespect, stealing, a variety of classroom disruptions (far from the old paper airplane days), weapons (previously discussed), and the list goes on.

Discipline problems can stem, too, from poverty, class and cultural differences, and wanting attention from parents. Newer philosophies and techniques such as restorative justice, positive behavioral inventions and supports, and trauma-informed and culturally responsive discipline practices are making a difference. Suffice it to say the life of a school leader is never dull and often stressful. Our respected school leader Luis, shared the following concerning managing unruly parents:

> Working in an urban elementary school comes with all kinds of safety concerns. I deal with unruly parents who are ready to settle things with fists rather than words. Being a respected school leader is about knowing those parents and knowing how to calm them down. It is also about cultivating relationships so [conflicts] do not get escalated.

Another respected school leader, Elena, clearly articulates where to begin when managing discipline. She said:

Sharing my core values and approach to discipline and how they align with our school and district's mission, vision, and values is essential to ensuring that our school community trusts that every decision will be consistently handled and with the individual student in mind. When navigating challenging disciplinary situations, our school community can trust that these guiding principles will inform every situation.

Technology

The technological revolution with social media has exponentially increased the challenges of school discipline. Some of us remember pretechnology school days and the first time computers appeared in our schools, dating back to the early 1980s. Rapidly evolving technology is profoundly and dramatically changing everyone's lives. Loubier (2021) stated the following concerning technology:

> Over the last centuries, society witnessed technological advancements gradually making everyday lives easier, more convenient, and – well, more interesting. In the 21st century, however, technology made a true quantum leap, with augmented reality, blockchain, artificial intelligence, and 3D printing being just a few examples of the most recent inventions.

As school leaders, we are challenged to use technology to improve student learning. Technology enhances our ability to personalize, individualize, and differentiate learning and generally improve students' experiences in schools. It is also employed to more efficiently and systematically assist with administrative tasks like communication, budgeting, and scheduling. It opens up a world of information with a keystroke –powerful, to say the least. While the benefits are numerous, our focus is on the challenges that give school leaders headaches and stress. Some of those school leader challenges, in no specific order, brought to us by way of technology are cyberbullying and harassment; cybersecurity from cyberattacks and threats to keeping data secure and information management; hiring and keeping up-to-date tech-savvy staff knowledgeable about curriculum, software, hardware, and appropriate usage; monitoring students with acceptable use policies to, for example, avoid plagiarism; ensuring fair and equitable access for all students; hardware and software maintenance from internet connectivity to having current platforms; professional development; and cell phone usage and nonusage.

Regulating the use or nonuse of cell phones can cause an array of classroom distractions and serious problems. Hatfield (2024) stated, "High school teachers are especially likely to see cellphones as problematic. About seven-in-ten (72%) say that students being distracted by cellphones is a major problem in their classroom, compared with 33% of middle school teachers and 6% of elementary school teachers." The *Los Angeles Times* Editorial Board (2024) stated:

> The 2024–25 school year may be the tipping point when adults act to curb kids' phone addiction and regain their attention. It's about time. It should be obvious by now that having a pocket-size entertainment center that constantly buzzes with alerts and enticements is not great for kids' ability to focus and learn. (It's not great for adults, either.) Simply having a phone nearby with notifications coming through can cause students to lose focus on the task at hand, according to one study. Once distracted, it can take as long as 20 minutes to re-focus. Other studies have found that keeping a phone close by during a lecture impairs attention and reduces memory retention.

To be fair, it is important to note that cell phones have recognizable educational benefits, such as accessing information and student collaboration. There is also the argument that cellphones can help keep students safer in case of an emergency. Working parents can keep in touch more easily if something arises at school, such as staying late. But the school leader needs to create the balance – a difficult one to achieve.

This list of challenges is enough to cause any school leader to stay up at night. And how about your personal privacy? Boucek (2024) said this about personal technology: "If you as a public employee do not want your grandmother to read it, don't speak it, don't text it, and don't do it" (p. 9). How to respond to a situation and how to communicate has become a mental task. The adage "think before you act" is now exponentially more critical.

Let's close this discussion on discipline with artificial intelligence. School leaders are charged with preparing our students for their future workplace. Artificial intelligence has been and will continue to be a life-altering game changer. Now, teachers have to deal with knowing whether a student's work is their own or was written by artificial intelligence. Bowen and Watson (2024) state:

> Generative AI is a different technology, and the way it is changing work is different too. While previous technological revolutions targeted the skilled but often manual jobs of factory workers, telephone operators, travel agents, and farmers, AI appears set to be more disruptive to lawyers, doctors, copywriters, insurance workers, insurance underwriters, translators, artists, and anyone who works with text.
>
> (p. 27)

From how to teach it to how to effectively manage it are all concerns for the school leader who struggles daily with the challenges of integrating technology. Respected school leaders know that every day will be hard work and have challenges. Respected school leader capital will help them. As our respected school leader Vanessa said, "Being respected makes hard work easier."

Budgetary Constraints

Technology is a big-buck industry! Shinde (2024) reported: "U.S. K-12 education technology spending pre-pandemic: Estimates suggest annual spending on education technology was between 26 billion and 41 billion." While the costs for up-to-date technology compete with scores of other items, school leaders know that the majority of a school's expenses are directed to employee salaries. The remaining monies have an array of competition, and technology is but one of them. This section discusses the challenges that competing expenditures bring to the table and how a school leader, when respected, is helped when migrating the challenging task of line-item allocation.

Our forefathers did not address education in the Constitution. Each of the fifty states has the responsibility for determining how public schools will be funded. Financing from state, local, and federal governments is the primary funding source. These sources vary significantly from state to state, and in states from school to school. Allegretto et al. (2022) reported,

> *Our current system for funding public schools shortchanges students, particularly low-income students.* Education funding generally is inadequate and inequitable; it relies too heavily on state and local resources (particularly property tax revenues), the federal government plays a small and an insufficient role, funding levels vary widely across states, and high-poverty districts get less funding per student than low-poverty districts.

After budgeting for fixed costs such as employee salaries and benefits; facility maintenance and utilities like gas, electricity, and water; capital outlay expenses; and transportation, there is little left for instruction, professional development, and other items that directly affect the quality of a student's education and the life of a teacher. While many school leaders have committees and various ways to receive input on remaining discretionary competing costs, ultimately, as they say, the buck stops with the school leader. In addition, when they say, "It's not about the money," well, you know it is! A school leader will take a hit if a staff member feels unfairly and/or disproportionately compensated when compared to another or receives less than one's fair share of instructional materials, supplies, and professional development dollars. A school leader needs to have great wisdom to survive. So how does being respected help?

Our respected school leader Vanessa, said, "I have a small budget, and I have to make strategic decisions on how to spend it. Knowing I am respected by my faculty, families, and local school council helps me because they trust me with the decisions I make on funding."

Luis needed more administrative assistance to support his students. He was like a broken record in not taking no for an answer when he advocated for his students. He finally got the assistant principal and special education case manager that he sorely needed. He said, "Do what you need in the moment, and it will come back to you. There is a level of respect for the job you do."

Elena used the extreme challenges of the pandemic to "take the time to allocate resources based on what was needed at the time. . . . The process I use is very collaborative." People will remember what you did in the very challenging times.

A school leader will never have enough money to create an ideal education for everyone. However, the respected school leader uses this challenge not only to be as collaborative as possible but also to be systematically decisive in decision-making, knowing that one can't please all the people all the time. One can only do the best and be as transparent as possible.

Constraints and Limitations From Contracts, Laws, Rules and Regulations, Court Rulings, and School District Policies

The lack of funding is a clear and present constraint and limitation on school leaders. When considering budgetary expenditures, depending on factors like school size and possible, probable, or pending litigation, one line item worth watching for being on the rise is school district legal fees. While many large school districts have law departments, some smaller districts have moved to having an attorney on staff. Legal challenges that confront school leaders can stem from federal, state, and local level laws, rules, and regulations, union and employee contracts, court rulings, and local school district policies. This assortment of areas creates a challenge caused by the constraints and limitations they place upon school leaders, limiting their flexibility and freedom to act on the job and the time spent for compliance. Contracts, laws, rules and regulations, court rulings, and local district policies are briefly discussed here.

Contracts. School leaders are responsible for the implementation and fidelity of contracts that govern teachers as well as numerous union and nonunion employees. Several unions can be involved in multiple negotiations resulting in multiple contracts requiring the school leader to be knowledgeable about a significant number of details for implementation. Failure to properly administer and manage the contract can result in grievances and lawsuits.

Laws, Rules and Regulations, and Court Rulings. Because public education is a function of the state, each state has its own laws, rules, and regulations spanning hundreds and hundreds of pages detailing everything from the number of school days in a year, hours per day to be spent on instruction, to the celebration or commemoration of specific holidays. Then you have the federal government via the U.S. Department of Education, covering the Every Student Succeeds Act (ESSA), civil rights, Family Education Rights and Privacy Act, Individuals with Disabilities Act (IDEA), and other topics. Couple that with all the federal court rulings, many by the Supreme Court, regarding freedom of speech or due process for student suspensions, and the list of school leaders' required knowledge goes on and on.

Local District Policies. Lastly, the school leader must follow local school board and district policies, which can include significant details regarding students, instruction, personnel, operations, and more. Use discretion – well, as much as possible – after everything else!

Staying up to date and administering the rules, laws, regulations, court rulings, and local policies can be overwhelming. But they are meant to bring fairness, equity, and consistency to the classroom. They also bring structure and routines as the answers to many questions can be found, and sometimes with needed legal advice. Being a respected school leader gives you a leg up in this challenging environment. One of our respected school leaders, Vanessa, said regarding needing minor changes to contract management and implementation, "If we have to do things differently in this challenging environment, we adjust. Because I am respected, we work out things together."

Regarding the complexity of managing schools, one of our respected school leaders, Elena, said:

> Education is about people, and our success as a school depends on the success of our students and staff. Being visible, present, and engrossed in the lives of the individuals I serve creates opportunities for support and encouragement. Developing and maintaining relationships is the foundation of any respected school leader.

One can tackle those challenging times by developing relationships.

There are many additional school leader challenges not included in this discussion that are certainly noteworthy, such as managing and navigating political winds and firestorms from book banning to prayer in schools to how to react to current events; closing the achievement gap; chronic absenteeism; the effects of poverty; teacher and staff shortages and managing the educator revolving door; developing curriculum; staff morale; parental under- and overinvolvement; professional development; work/life balance and dealing with stress; staying physically and emotionally healthy; and, of course, the well-being of students, which was given its own chapter. This is a partial list of those not covered – just some of those endless, time-consuming challenges school leaders are required to manage frequently. Reading the list alone probably causes stress!

Then, there is an obvious one for any student- and staff-centered principal: the incredible amount of time spent managing and responding to the concerns that arise in the complicated daily life of students and staff – some very serious, like student, staff, and parental health issues, to minor ones, like "the dog (now the computer) ate my homework." School leaders are called upon to prevent and resolve problems and, in doing so, act as counselors, clergy, and comforters to students, faculty, and parents. Some days, a school leader may feel like Sisyphus, constantly pushing the boulder uphill, only to start over again (Cuyler, n.d.). Your currency as a school leader is the amount of time you have each day to lead. Challenges consume a lot of that much-needed currency. But when tackled with dignity, honor, and intelligence, those challenges can advance your respected school leader status.

For the daily barrage of challenges brought to the principal for advice or just an ear, our respected school leader Vanessa said,

> One of the things I have is an open-door policy. Often . . . they will plop themselves down on a chair by my desk. I say, "Do you want me to listen or respond?" Sometimes, they just want to cry. Frequently, they just want to be heard. It is transparent, and they know that; I have built camaraderie, trust, and respect, and we can have these conversations.

Now, let's go back to the beginning of this chapter with Vanessa. Shots fired present one of the most challenging moments for even a career veteran administrator to manage. While the situation for Vanessa resulted in "managing" the school after the event and not dealing with a person physically injured, she had to deal with the fallout from that situation and its time-consuming nature. We close this chapter with a case study from our respected school leader John. It demonstrates the incredible complexity and the spiraling-out-of-control nature of what can happen when a student thinks he is making a seemingly innocuous comment that could be an incredibly disconcerting and dangerous one. It also demonstrates the benefits that come with being a respected school leader.

Case Study

> This is how I remember the event, and I may get some of the exact details wrong, but for the most part, this is what happened. I had a special education student who I will

call Tommy. He was socially awkward, sometimes staring at students in the cafeteria and having a hard time understanding social cues. Some students called him awkward. They were not malicious and did not bully or ridicule him, but I am sure there were some sidebar conversations. This opinion was formed after I spoke to many students.

One Saturday, Tommy is trying to catch up on a homework assignment. He calls his friend Jimmy (not his real name), on a Saturday night as he is trying to get help to finish. When he gets the assistance he needs, he makes an inappropriate comment like, "If I were going to shoot up the school, I would not target you." Later on, when we interviewed him, he told us he was just trying to act cool and in no way meant it as a threat. At the time, he was trying to express his thanks as best he could and express how he felt about his friendship with Jimmy.

Now this is the timeline of events from Saturday night at 10:00 p.m. until Monday morning.

Tommy makes the statement to Jimmy, who awkwardly laughs. Jimmy shares this story with another friend, who shares it on and on for half the night through group chats and phone calls. A vicious "telephone" game reenacted.

On Sunday morning, parents get wind of the story, which has now morphed into Tommy having multiple weapons and planning to shoot up the school on Monday. He has a list of students, especially students in his fifth-period class and one young girl who he outwardly likes. The tagline on many of these group chats is: "Are you on his list?"

Our school has a policy of "See Something, Say Something," so everyone's phones are blowing up. Teachers, staff members, board members, other students, and mine. I wake up Sunday morning to 89 text messages. Parents are irate. Many parents have decided to keep their children home on Monday because [they feel] the administration does not care, primarily caring about public image, so they are not reprimanding the student especially considering he is a special education student. Students planned a safety walkout, which they did a week later and was covered by the news. By the way, the news quoted students, not the facts! It was a mess on my end; however, it was not nearly as bad as for Tommy, who was now getting threats from other students. His mom, in tears, and I were constantly talking about what can be done. Monday morning arrives, and this is now full-blown. I called the central office, who I have been in contact with since Sunday, and updated them on the situation. They told me they were aware of this and sent us safety and security leadership to assist us with this situation. I asked them to craft an email to quell the situation, which took about four hours to get because it had to be vetted by at least 10–15 people, including lawyers and communications. (The good news is now the central office has pre-vetted letters available to help us offset the gossip and fear before it can get legs and are ready to go in a few minutes). This situation is now full-blown, and the rumor mill has Tommy walking to school now because some students saw him carrying a rifle to school. Yeah . . . it got that crazy. I received the news as I was talking to Tommy's mom on the phone while Tommy was standing next to her at home.

I am not allowed to distribute an email to anyone until I get permission, so my admin team and I are walking the hallways calmly telling everyone we see that everything is fine and it's just a bad rumor.

I finally received a vetted and approved email around 1:30 p.m., which I sent to all our stakeholders. Everyone's trust in us took a hit, thinking we were slow in our actions, inattentive, or dismissive. I had a meeting the next day after school to discuss what happened. I explained that our hands were tied, and we did all we could do. I know my role as a respected leader did help in three ways.

First, only about half of our faculty showed up at the after-school meeting. When I questioned some who did not attend, some said they had appointments or family obligations, and since the meeting was not mandatory, they figured they could find out what happened at the meeting from colleagues the next day. Many missing faculty members told me, "We knew you had it handled, and I was not worried." I have gained a sort of reverent respect from my staff, community, and families. Second, in the end, around 80% of my teachers and family members thought we did a great job given the constraints we had to wrestle with; 95% of our students felt reassured. Lastly, we used this instance as a learning moment, which was valued because I was respected. I spoke to the students and explained how you "See something, say something." That you just don't use the internet and let it get out of control. You call an adult first and let them know so we can discover the truth, try to control the situation, and not feed the rumor mill. We always share this message too at the beginning of the year.

John, a veteran and respected school leader, has a crystal-clear view of challenging times. He also shared the following words of wisdom for us to pause and reflect. "I am in no way comparing myself to our country's greatest leaders. I want to make that clear. When you look at what many people consider our most respected leaders, they tend to all have led during some of our most trying times. Washington during the Revolutionary War, Lincoln during the Civil War, and Roosevelt during the Great Depression. Maybe some respect was bestowed upon them because of the times in which they led. Difficult times are the fertilizer that feeds the Respect Tree. With that said, maybe I benefited from three strikes and work stoppages, a worldwide pandemic, a $74 million new Freshman Academy, and an increase of students from 3000 to 4400. Throw in a bout of Leukemia, pneumonia, and a few ancillary heart attacks, and maybe my respect was fertilized by these trials and tribulations."

Reflection Questions:

Q1 Think of your ideal "safe" school. Now place it on a scale from 1 (all open access) to 10 (a complete lockdown atmosphere with outside perimeter security). A school leader is challenged to pick that number and create that balance. What is your number? What factors did you use to determine it?

Q2 As our respected school leader John, said, "Difficult times are the fertilizer that feeds the Respect Tree." Reflecting on the "fertilizer" you have experienced, how is your tree doing? What kind of tree would you be?

Q3 How do you stay healthy, manage stress, and keep a work-life balance?

References

Allegretto, S., García, E., & Weiss, E. (2022, July 12). *Public education funding in the U.S. needs an overhaul*. Economic Policy Institute. https://www.epi.org/publication/public-education-funding-in-the-us-needs-an-overhaul/

Banerji, O., & Mallon, S. (2024, July 31). Active shooter drills that prepare but don't traumatize: Advice from principals. *Education Week*. https://www.edweek.org/leadership/active-shooter-drills-that-prepare-but-dont-traumatize-advice-from-principals/2024/07

Boucek, S. (2024, August 1). Employee privacy on personal technology. *School Administrator*. https://www.aasa.org/resources/resource/employee-privacy-personal-technology

Bowen, J., & Watson, C. (2024). *Teaching with AI: A practical guide to a new era of human learning*. John Hopkins University Press.

Bultinck, H., & Bush, L. (2009). *99 ways to lead and succeed: Strategies and stories for school leaders*. Eye on Education.

Cox, J., Rich, S., Trevor, L., Muyskens, J., & Ulmanu, M. (2024, September 6). More than 383,000 students have experienced gun violence at school since Columbine. *Washington Post.* https://www.washingtonpost.com/education/interactive/school-shootings-database/

Cuyler, C. (n.d.). *The myth of Sisyphus.* The Pilgrims' School. Retrieved August 27, 2024, from https://www.thepilgrims-school.co.uk/the-myth-of-sisyphus

Forbes, M. (n.d.). Retrieved August 1, 2024, from https://parade.com/1012592/kelseypelzer/quotes-for-tough-times/

Hatfield, J. (2024, June 12). *72% of U.S. high school teachers say cellphone distraction is a major problem in the classroom.* Pew Research Centre. https://www.pewresearch.org/short-reads/2024/06/12/72-percent-of-us-high-school-teachers-say-cellphone-distraction-is-a-major-problem-in-the-classroom/

Law Insider. (n.d.). *Violent incident.* Retrieved August 7, 2024, from https://www.lawinsider.com/dictionary/violent-incident

Los Angeles Times Editorial Board. (2024, August 19). Yes, more schools should ban school cell phones. *Los Angeles Times*, p. A8.

Loubier, A. (2021, December 10). Is society moving in the right direction with technology rapidly taking over the world? *Forbes.* https://www.forbes.com/sites/andrealoubier/2021/06/01/is-society-moving-in-the-right-direction-with-technology-rapidly-taking-over-the-world/

Maslow, A. H. (2013). *A theory of human motivation.* Martino.

National Center for Education Statistics. (2024). *Crime, violence, discipline, and safety in U.S. public schools.* https://nces.ed.gov/pubs2024/2024043.pdf

National Center on Safe Supportive Learning Environments. (n.d.). *Discipline.* https://safesupportivelearning.ed.gov/topic-research/environment/discipline

Shinde, Y. (2024, March 6). *K-12 education technology spend market grow USD 132.4 billion by 2032.* Market.us Scoop. https://scoop.market.us/k-12-education-technology-spend-market-grow-usd-132-4-bn-by-2032/

7
School Leader Self-Respect

There are so many "self" words in our vocabulary that we use to describe our everyday life, like *selfies, self-employed, self-taught*, and *self-disciplined*, just to name a few that have positive connotations. And then there are some other "self" words, like *self-defense, self-centered*, and *self-righteous* that may have negative undertones. Whatever the "self" word, the prefix "self" is about YOU; therefore, this chapter is about YOU and your self-respect. My what? Your self-respect and how it benefits you in being respected as a school leader.

Self-respect is sometimes used interchangeably with self-esteem in professional literature. While the two words are related, they appear to have different, notable characteristics. Michael Smith (2023) explains the difference in his article "Self-Respect and Self-Esteem: Twin Pillars of Personal Growth":

- ♦ Self-Esteem: This refers to our overall sense of self-worth and how we value ourselves. It's often influenced by external factors such as achievements, recognition, and validation from others. A person with high self-esteem feels confident in their abilities and worth.
- ♦ Self-Respect: This goes beyond mere self-perception. It's about how we treat ourselves, the boundaries we set, and demanding respect from

others. Unlike self-esteem, which can fluctuate based on external validation, self-respect remains more constant and is rooted in our core values.

(p. 8)

Additionally, self-respect has a strong moral foundation underlying our behavior in our lives as well as contributing to a meaningful life worth living (Dillon, 2022). For example, watching a sports player argue, shout, and cuss face-to-face a referee or umpire and then be tossed out of the game indicates a behavior that crosses the line, as no respectful person should act that way to another, nor should the person listening to the words accept them or put up with them. Therefore, self-respect is based on our values and beliefs, and it prioritizes our well-being. It is more than feeling good for the moment, being right, and getting your way. It is a larger path into the future than one moment of how we treat ourselves. Therefore, self-respect is not dependent on outside validation of others as it is dependent internally on who we are and what we say to ourselves as to what we can and cannot do daily. Or as simply said by Brene Brown (2018, p. 164), "Who we are is how we lead."

Self-respect is an influencer like YouTube, Facebook, and musical star Taylor Swift. It may guide us and become an agent for our school leadership behavior to make decisions that are aligned with personal and organizational values and beliefs. This influence also filters others as they feel respected, supported, and can accomplish their tasks. It can translate to trust in others which allows the school organization to move toward greater results (Meshanko, 2013).

Respected school principal Luis, stated, "Self-respect is knowing who you are and where you want to go." That is influence, courage, and impact, as stated by a respected school leader, and allows him to choose a direction and focus for the school. Other benefits of self-respect for the respected school leader are that others can follow your leadership and trust your decisions because of who you are. In the parent survey for one of the respected school leaders, Vanessa, one parent commented, "You will be able to talk with the principal the first day of school." That direct and succinct statement from a parent makes it clear that the principal can make an impression by positively or negatively influencing this parent contact immediately on the first day of school. In Vanessa's case, it was a positive, approachable influence.

Earning self-respect is not putting oneself before others to feel good such as making test scores look better than they really are by presenting only partial data to stakeholders (acting against one's value of honesty). It is not about developing your ego, arrogance, or self-importance. Self-respect is not concerned with how others perceive you, hoping for their approval and confirmation, although some school leaders might confuse constant approval and confirmation with valid feedback. Constant approval could be a behavior that would fall in the self-esteem area because it is influenced by external factors. For the school leader who is a people pleaser, meaning the leader likes to make sure students, faculty, parents, and the community are happy and their needs are met, this behavior, while admirable, can be all-consuming. Remember the old saying "You can't please all the people all the time." Usually, the school leader ends up not pleasing everyone and feeling guilty about what more they could have done or giving it one last best shot (Bultinck & Bush, 2009). Guilt on the overtime clock can slip unconsciously into one's self-respect because of the worry that everyone's needs are not met.

Think of self-respect daily when practicing personal leadership skills. If you have brushed off not considering how you treat yourself because others come first, then it is time to take action on your personal and professional development. Attending a conference here or there will not do it. Self-respect can be seen as growth over time, and you have a lifetime, but not thinking about self-respect can limit your satisfaction with how you are currently doing your work of leading, which clearly affects everyone else. Think of self-respect as an attitude that might need adjusting. For example, maybe you are a school leader who is always available to whomever by phone or email 24/7. You are on demand. While that behavior is commendable, it is also exhausting and draining. Possibly new, healthy adjustments need to be made by communicating when and how you will return phone calls and emails, not leaving stakeholders wondering and wanting instant responses. Think of self-respect as an ability to see the potential of this gift and listen to yourself, know yourself, appreciate yourself, and express yourself.

Listen to Yourself

During a school day, how often do you think about the behaviors you experience? Probably not often. There is happiness in seeing students coming to school and beginning their day, joyfulness in the opportunities and adventures students will experience in learning, watching students congregating with their classmates, and the pleasure in watching the interaction of a skillful teacher and students in the teaching/learning process in the classroom, just to provide a few examples. Sometimes there is the annoyance of a student who has been told to stop pushing other students and keeps doing it in your presence or a teacher who has been asked several times by the principal to stand in the hall by their classroom door to greet students prior to class beginning just like the other teachers – but the teacher is not there when you walk by. The point of this is that certain behaviors trigger reactions in most human beings, and school leaders experience a multitude of behaviors on a daily basis, such as students giving you a hug, showing you their 100 percent score on a test, or asking you how you liked the win at the volleyball game last night. Other behaviors you may have experienced are students swearing or parents' finger-pointing or finger-waving in your face while threatening to have you fired. Another example is a teacher who likes to disagree with you in public using a faculty meeting as the venue. These positive and negative behaviors trigger reactions in you and most school leaders have a mental plan of how to handle these situations because it is under their control (Cloud, 2013, p. 160).

School leaders are masterful actors, and most can ignore personal behaviors that bother them and remain calm, cool, and collected. (Bultinck & Bush, 2009, p. 62) However, sometimes there are clues that a school leader is upset.

Here is a true story: At a monthly school board meeting, the superintendent was dealing with changing a school boundary area for the fall school year to equalize student attendance at several schools. A group of parents in the areas affected by the boundary change asked to speak at the meeting. Each person spoke or, in some cases, shouted for their allotted time of three minutes, expressing their opinions and calling out the superintendent. The school leader remained calm, cool, and collected as the attacking comments continued person after person. However, as time went on, the neck of the superintendent began to turn bright pink, then red, and the color kept rising throughout the face, forehead, and into the hairline. The nonverbal signs were telling a different story than the calm superintendent sitting and listening. Obviously, this leader was upset and showing signs of being agitated. The superintendent should not be faulted for this physical reaction, but it is a reminder that we cannot hide all our feelings, and this leader was not aware of the rising color that was happening in the skin. While many school leaders can control external behavior like facial expression, eye gestures, posture, or remain silent, internal behavior can reveal a different story.

The moral of this story is that school leaders should be aware of the leadership behaviors they exhibit and can control. They should value those that they are working on to be a successful, respected school leader. In the story, everyone at the board meeting was wondering what would happen next. It is easy to lose your composure when you are being criticized. You should think about what is going well in the school and realize what you are able to control (Wingate & Schneider, 2024). Are there behaviors that prompt reactions inside of you? Here is a quick way to take an inventory of your behaviors and begin giving yourself the time you deserve.

Looking at the My Leadership Behaviors Chart, on the left there is a space for you to write about the leadership behaviors that you feel you have attained and valued. Next are some examples of admirable leadership behaviors. On the right, write about leadership behaviors you are working on. Some leadership behavior examples are provided that you might consider.

TABLE 7.1 My Leadership Behaviors

I value in me	Examples	I am working on	Examples
	Hard worker		Calmness
	Good communicator		Listening
	Organized		Asking for help
	Problem solver		More visibly
	Accountable		Let it go!

If you listen to yourself, you will know when certain leadership behaviors mean you can give yourself a pat on the back and others may cause you to pause, rethink, and/or reset.

Sandberg (2013) talks about the internal barriers that could stop you from developing self-respect, like fear of failing in the job or task, being hard on yourself when things do not go right, becoming vulnerable and taking chances, settling for being liked rather than respected, or putting self-respect on hold – just not thinking about it. These fears demonstrate a lack of self-confidence going forward and as Sandberg points out, it can be a self-fulfilling prophecy in that one could do more if only one could put this lack of confidence aside (p. 33). Furthermore, Sandberg explains that self-doubt can become self-defense, which can downplay one's abilities and achievements (p. 33). One example that comes to mind is a new school leader who has a high school teaching background but is now a principal in a middle school or elementary school. The new leader may fear that their high school experience may not transfer to the middle or elementary school and, at first, may fear they have too much to learn on the job and will not have credibility with the staff. However, an adjustment can be made by not underestimating oneself and practicing one's valued leadership behaviors. After all, the school leader was hired for the position for the leadership strengths they possess.

Additionally, Ward and Meyer (2018) support school leaders who practice self-respect by stating they will "experience greater composure, confidence, and satisfaction at work and in life" (p. 102). Elena, one of our respected school leaders, commented, "Self-respect gives me the confidence to continue. It gives me the courage to take on more." She gave a clear example of what this looks like for her in the following statement.

> As an equity-focused leader, I take on the responsibility of raising awareness through research on topics that adversely affect minoritized student populations. During the year, I partnered with our superintendent to lead a presentation for other school principals on language differences versus learning disabilities as we actively work to strengthen our MTSS process. Although some topics are complex to speak of, such as the overidentification of [English language learners] as having learning disabilities, my self-respect gives me the confidence and courage to take on these leadership responsibilities.

There are ways to avoid behavior barriers to self-respect and work toward its development. Some of these suggestions might already be incorporated into your daily life, so in that case, it could be a review, and for others, the ideas might be new. Here are some ideas:

- Let it go! If behavior triggers upset you, put the negative energy you feel toward people or situations aside. What is in the past is in the past! Rather than reliving, replaying, and reviewing what happened, take the energy spent and apply it to a change in positive behavior for yourself. Just move on (Bultinck & Bush, 2009, p. 82; Meshanko, 2013, p. 139).
- Turn negativity into positivity by addressing fear and anxiety with a statement such as, "What adventure or new learning am I going to experience today?" This thought can be applied to meeting your new doctor for the first time, interviewing for a school leadership job, or

presenting at a national conference, to name a few examples (Sandberg, 2013).
- ◆ Take the time to develop and practice self-respect. The more it is practiced, the more it becomes a natural part of YOU.

Know Yourself

When the workday is over for you, is it really over? Do you ever wonder how you got home since your mind was reviewing school tasks to be done and you don't remember anything about driving because driving home was a blur? It sounds like your workday is overflowing into your home life, whether you realize it or not. How do you balance your work and home life? (Bultinck & Bush, 2009, p. 67). Is your balance off? "Work/life balance" refers to "one's involvement and engagement in work and nonwork life presented with minimal conflict between the two roles," according to Sirgy and Lee (2018). Yet the conflict is challenging and has not diminished for those who are school leaders.

Jeff Haring (2016), in an article entitled "Helping School Leaders Find Life Balance," comments on how difficult it is for school leaders to ever get caught up, and urges administrators to find the sweet spot, that place where one can relieve the stress of the school workday and not have the work leak into one's home life. However, every administrator's home life is different, such as a principal who has small children at home or a principal who is taking care of an elderly relative. Therefore, school leaders need to build a culture of life balance to ensure the retention of school leaders and avoid burnout. One suggestion that stood out in the article was clarifying urgent tasks such as, "This report needs to be completed, but it does not have to be perfect. Just get it in on time." Another idea was letting principals take the afternoon off to work on critical reports such as teacher evaluations while other central office personnel are on call to the school.

The research on work-life balance for school leaders began in just this decade. However, the work on teacher well-being has been steadily growing over the past 10 years, as evidenced by a comprehensive review of studies by Benjamin Dreer (2023). Included in this review of 76,990 teachers and 44 studies is the concern for the characteristics of teacher well-being. Characteristics such as sleep quality, teacher retention, and teacher/student relationships are a few of the characteristics addressed in some of the studies he examined. Three conclusions and recommendations he suggested were that more work needs to be done to pinpoint the links between teachers' home and work lives and specific personal and professional outcomes. Could this research shed light on school leaders' well-being characteristics as well?

Other literature published on school leader well-being is noteworthy. One study of 473 active, practicing building administrators in Arkansas by Ray et al. (2020) produced some significant results to consider. Through survey questions to these principal participants, the researchers investigated the well-being areas of sleep deprivation, nutrition, hydration, exercise, and the role of mindfulness and social engagement as a strategy for coping with stress. The study revealed that compared to the general population in the literature, school administrators are working longer hours, sleeping less, rarely exercising, sacrificing time with loved ones, and missing out on activities outside of their jobs that bring them meaning and joy (p. 442).

Here is more detail. While each area of well-being studied produced general conclusions, other factors were uncovered that affected the self-care and self-respect of school leaders as well as their behavior and practice. Here are some interesting conclusions from the school leader participants:

- 40 percent of the participants were sleep deprived, sleeping less than the average American who gets seven hours (Hirshkowitz et al., 2015).
- 62 percent of the participants were at least 15 pounds overweight.

- 80 percent of the participants go one day a week without any meals during their workday.
- 80 percent of the participants are not getting enough water.
- 86 percent of the participants get less than the recommended cardiovascular exercise.
- 47 percent of the participants never engage in meditative practices.
- 80 percent of the participants spend less than three hours a day with their family.
- 44 percent respondents knew very little about their role to promote self-care.
- Over 50 percent felt incapable of changing the administrative role to accommodate their personal needs.
- Participants worked 16.55 hours per week more than the average American.

The percentages in this study speak for themselves. Most school leaders know what they should be doing to respect and care for themselves but often choose not to follow through for a variety of reasons. One reason suggested in the study might be that some leaders believe that ignoring their own health really means performing their job at the highest level because others need to see them as servant leaders or being the ultimate accountable authority. The authors of this study named this school leader the "sacrificial school leader," whose success comes from being selfless in the eyes of others but, over time, realize this behavior is not sustainable. This sounds like the leader is looking to build self-esteem rather than self-respect. One powerful comment in the study suggested that "although many school leaders believe they are giving their students, schools, and communities their all, they are likely not giving them their best."

To be at your best by not sacrificing time for yourself and putting self-respect aside does not make sense in school leadership and is actually counterproductive. This general deficiency in self-care and respect produces a false sense of success and erodes one's self-respect practices to the point of exhaustion, unhealthy behaviors, and burnout (Cloud, 2013, p. 222).

Express Yourself

It's time – maybe way past time – to set up boundaries at work. The pandemic, although a huge challenge, was helpful in many ways, and one of those ways was to allow us to think differently about our interactions with our work and make critical changes that might not have happened otherwise. For example, some teachers experienced changes in classroom time structure from working solely in the classroom to working online, to working in a hybrid situation – both online and in the classroom – and finally back to working solely in the traditional classroom. Educators make decisions on what classroom time look like. The pandemic made educators think about the best use of classroom time to meet the needs of all students. And that should be an ongoing, evaluative discussion all the time. As the traditional structuring of classroom time has undergone changes for the better because of educator conversation, did school leader work time have the same opportunity for conversation in the postpandemic years?

That depends on you. Did you make any changes or create any new boundaries at work when you had the chance in the new postpandemic normal? No one but you can set the boundaries for you (Brown, 2015, 2018; Cloud, 2013; Norville, 2009). Possibly you decided to expand your professional network as you discovered new support systems while creatively solving problems with technological tools. This establishes a new boundary for doing work using tools that other administrators may not be using. Possibly you have decided to rein in parents who are negatively interacting with you by respectfully taking back control over situations, revising your behavior, and practicing self-respect by not letting it upset you to the extent it did in the past.

Don't forget that standing up to criticism and judgment is done in a respectful, humble manner with a strong sense of self. One can hear the words and not let the words disturb one. The school leader has a strong confidence foundation in their strengths and the values that they bring to the school organization and then look forward to ways to learn, grow, and expand them (Chatsworth, 2017).

Express yourself by finding out how you are perceived by others (Meshanko, 2013, p. 68). The feedback process could be as short as a face-to-face conversation or as large as a survey of all the stakeholders in the school community. This exercise is not meant to be a formal evaluation but to test the waters of how you affected a particular event, such as graduation, state testing, a professional development day, or a procedure such as modes of communication to parents or designing traffic lanes for cars arriving at school. Some school leaders might naturally shy away from such an idea by saying they already know the answer or that the time is not right to ask for input. In any case, what leaders are really saying is they don't want to put themselves in such a vulnerable place, or they are fearful and defensive of what others might say. The reward for asking for feedback is the gift of building trust and not assuming you have all the answers. Brené Brown (2018) frames the feedback idea as a challenge by asking if, as a school leader, you are brave enough to listen (p. 203). Dr. Henry Cloud (2013) states:

> The process of staying in touch, whether with those above you, below you, around you, outside the organization, or the customers, should always be in the spirit of service. It should be done to find out how to serve them better, what they need from you, and what you need from them to serve the mission itself.
>
> (p. 219)

The respected school leaders in this book allow themselves to be vulnerable by asking students, teachers, parents, and the community for feedback about various aspects of their leadership. Their self-respect is expanded with honest, productive, and personal feedback. The evidence suggests how they can apply what they learn to become a better leader, confirming how their energy paid off while enjoying the work of school leadership – leading, learning, and growing.

Appreciate Yourself

How do you honor yourself? Remembering it is not about ego, arrogance, or self-importance. Are you fair and honest with yourself, or are you continually distracted, putting out fires and pushing self-respect aside? The job of leading a school is only one thing about you, although a critical one, but there is so much more. As Michael Jackson sang in his song "The Man in the Mirror," a clear message is sent to the listener. Why not take the time to look at yourself in a mirror, and if you don't like what you see, make a change? Here are a few more ideas to help you appreciate yourself:

- Write a letter to yourself at the beginning of the school year and talk about your professional goals at work and personal self-respect goals. Pull the letter out each quarter of the school year and review it. Adjust as necessary. When you retire you might pull them all out.
- Imagine yourself as your best respected school leader self and begin to show up as that person and see what happens.
- Check your stamina and energy levels. Are you taking care of yourself physically, mentally, and emotionally as you take care of others? (Kristenson, 2022)
- Plan your summer vacation.

You need stamina and energy to be of service to others (Kristenson, 2022). In fact, you might want to think about time management as energy and stamina management. This idea is not so much about the time it takes to do a task but the energy and stamina involved. For example, how much time does it take to do a teacher evaluation versus how much energy/stamina is involved when you have to do 30 teacher evaluations? Scheduling time with each teacher and managing the energy it takes to complete the teacher evaluation process might be double trouble. It might take many hours to complete the visits with a teacher and write up the evaluation. Certainly, reviewing and discussing a teacher's work should be an exciting and rewarding time for both the teacher and the school leader. Yet under pressure and deadlines, it can be a dreaded task that is hurried and superficial for both involved.

If you like making lists and crossing things off, that can be a sign of being productive during the day and might make you feel good about the physical act of crossing things off as you review the list at the end of the day. However, imagine there is an invisible, mental, "list supervisor" who comes along, assesses the list, and is concerned with: 1) What goes on the list? 2) Is the list ever completed? 3) Do unfinished items from the day before go to the top of the new list for the next day? 4) As the list grows, is there frustration that little is being crossed off? Is the list causing stress? 5) Does the list eventually get lost or tossed out? Yes, lists can be helpful and useful if you are a school leader who manages lists efficiently and effectively, but they can also be stress producers for a number of reasons, as mentioned previously.

You should appreciate that you know the difference between which leadership energy excites you, such as working on the school budget, and which energy drains you, such as strategic planning. As expected, school leaders cannot pick and choose which required tasks to do or not to do; however, a healthy self-respect approach can foster the best positive effort by being upfront about yourself.

Winning the Self-Respect Lottery: Cashing in on the Benefit of Self-Respect Toward Personal Success

The daunting work of leading a school organization is, in large part, understanding who you are as a leader or, in simple terms, demonstrating your leadership identity or styles in that setting (Altman, 2022). It is more than who you think you are or who you want to be. A respected school leader has a confident moral foundation of values that allows one to build on one's strengths and be open to growth and improvement in weaker leadership areas. When you honestly know who you are as a leader, you become immune to harsh criticism, insults, and lack of civility from others. Self-respect is on display every day, whether the leader is conscious or unconscious of it.

There is even more value to leadership work when you respect yourself and can cash in on the benefits. Without a school leader's self-respect, a respectful school is doubtful. How is it possible for a school leader to meet so many human needs in a school when they are not able to meet their own personal needs? If leaders cannot respect themselves, they surely will reveal behaviors to others that are unpleasant, such as anger, frustration, fear, or apathy (Meshanko, 2013, p. 193). Therefore, self-respect starts with being present for you. Think of respect as a blanket that comforts you when situations are difficult and gives you time to become resilient and call on your energy reserve. It includes listening to ourselves, knowing ourselves, expressing ourselves, and appreciating ourselves for the leadership work we do as a school leader working toward our best leader: "self."

In an informal interview, John, one of our respected school leaders, talks about how he knows himself, expresses himself, and appreciates himself while displaying leadership characteristics as a caring, collaborative, optimistic, and supportive principal for his students. His earned self-respect and respect as a school leader have allowed him to be successful.

> I am an expert on my high school's community. I went to a private high school and taught at a selective high school. Students are under stress to make critical choices about where they go to high school. My school was not in the conversations about students who were college bound, so I knew the game about the private schools versus the selective schools versus the neighborhood schools. I talked about the pros and cons of each and how my school was a neighborhood school, safe with an IB diploma, and let people make their own decisions. In essence, I can speak the language of my community. I knew I had arrived when the police and fire department employees sent their children to my high school. The kids thanked me at graduation and said they had made the right choice.

Reflection Questions:

Q1 What grade would you give yourself as you think about your self-respect?
Q2 How do you honor your self-respect on a daily basis?

References

Altman, D. (2022, February 20). *4 sure-fire ways to boost your self-awareness*. Center for Creative Leadership. https://www.ccl.org/articles/leading-effectively-articles/4-ways-boost-self-awareness/

Brown, B. (2015). *Rising strong: How the ability to reset, transforms the way we live, parent and Live.* Spiegel and Grace.

Brown, B. (2018). *Dare to lead: Brave work, tough conversations, whole hearts.* Random House.

Bultinck, H., & Bush, L. (2009). *99 ways to lead and succeed: Stories and strategies for school leaders.* Eye on Education.

Chatsworth Consulting Group. (2017, February 28). *Why self-respect is a key leadership skill.* https://www.chatsworthconsulting.com/2017/02/28/why-self-respect-is-a-key-leadership-skill

Cloud, H. (2013). *Boundaries for leaders.* HarperCollins Publishers.

Dillon, R. S. (2022, July 2). Respect. In E. N. Zalta & U. Nodelman (Eds.), *Stanford Encyclopedia of Philosophy archive.* https://plato/standord/edu/archives/fall2022/entries/respect/

Dreer, B. (2023). On the outcomes of teacher wellbeing: A systematic review of research. *Frontiers in Psychology, 14,* Article 1205179. https://doi.org/10.3389/fpsyg.2023.1205179

Haring, J. (2016). https://thesuccessfulprincipal.org/uploads/7/5/8/0/75800261/helping_leaders_find_balance_-_harding_-_2016.pdf

Hirshkowitz, M., Whiton, K., Albert, S. M., Alessi, C., Bruni, O., DonCarlos, L., Hazen, N., Herman, J., Katz, E. S., Kheirandish-Gozal, L., Neubauer, D. N., O'Donnell, A. E., Ohayon, M., Peever, J., Rawding, R., Sachdeva, R. C., Setters, B., Vitiello, M. V., Ware, J. C., & Adams Hillard, P. J. (2015). National Sleep Foundation's sleep time duration recommendations: Methodology and results summary. *Sleep Health, 1*(1), 40–43. https://doi.org/10.1016/j.sleh.2014.12.010

Kristenson, S. (2022, February 10). 13 ways to show respect for others in everyday life. *Happierhuman.com*. www.happierhuman.com/show-respect/

Meshanko, P. (2013). *The respect effect*. McGraw-Hill.

Norville, D. (2009). *The power of respect*. Thomas Nelson.

Ray, J., Pijanowski, J., & Lasater, K. (2020). The self-care practices of school principals. *Journal of Educational Administration*, *58*(4), 435–451. https://doi.org/10.1108/JEA-04-2019-0073

Sandberg, S. (2013). *Lean in*. Alfred A. Knopf.

Sirgy, M., & Lee, D. (2018). Work-life balance: An integrative review. *Applied Research in Quality of Life*, *13*(1), 229–254. https://doi.org/10.1007/s11482-017-9509-8

Smith, M. (2023, August 20). *Self-respect and self-esteem: Twin pillars of personal growth*. Self-Esteem Generator. https://selfesteemgenerator.com/self-respect/

Ward, G., & Meyer, W. G. (2018). *The respectful leader: Seven ways to influence without intimidation: A business fable*. Winding Creek Press.

Wingate, B., & Schneider, M. (2024, April 6). *How to make servant leadership more sustainable? Balance self and others*. Center for Creative Leadership. https://www.ccl.org/articles/leading-effectively-articles/how-to-make-servant-leadership-more-sustainable-by-balancing-self-others/

8

A School Leader: Respected and Transformational

Definition and Background

There are numerous leadership styles for a school leader to choose from depending on vision, mission, goals, situations, and stakeholder involvement. Their potential, merit, impact, and usefulness will affect the desired outcomes. This chapter focuses on transformational leadership as a different way of leading: a more dynamic, rewarding, and purposeful approach for leaders and followers, and its relationship to being a respected school leader. At first glance, the term *transformational* suggests change, coming from the root word *transform*; however, this leadership style proposes an even deeper, detailed meaning.

In 1973, sociologist Downton (1973) presented the idea of transformational leadership as a way to analyze the relationship between leaders and followers involving leadership styles and political movements such as the Black Muslims and Bolsheviks (Downton, 1973). Building on the idea from Downton, Burns (1978) discussed the difficulty in distinguishing between management and leadership and noted that the differences appear to be in the characteristics and behavior of the individual.

Most experts cite Burns (2012) as the person who defined transformational leadership as "when one or more persons engage with

DOI: 10.4324/9781003296201-8

others in such a way that leaders and followers raise one another to higher levels of motivation and morality" (p. 37). In other words, when a group of people come together there is a natural leader-follower relationship that takes place (Van Vugt, 2006). The early editions of *Bass and Stogdill's Handbook of Leadership* (Bass, 1990) cite research on personal traits, attributes, values, and tendencies that differentiate leaders from the group. The research compared competitiveness and risk-taking by the leader as well as the followers moving toward the feeling of esteem toward the leader. In later research, leader traits were categorized into four specific behavior components. These behavioral components are known as the Four I's. The Four I's form a behavioral framework and are even more powerful when combined (Bass & Avolio, 1994; Clarinal, 2021; Lindberg, 2022; Ugochukwu, 2021). They are as follows.

1. Individualized Consideration. Leaders serve as mentors or coaches to followers and attend to their needs by listening and offering empathy and support. Mutual respect and admiration are necessary means of celebrating the followers' contributions, personal development, and self-growth.
2. Individualized Influence. Leaders serve as role models and are trusted and respected. Followers want to emulate the leader. They can rally individuals around a shared vision and are able to listen, focus, and center others on the present moment.
3. Inspirational Motivation. Leaders serve as positive motivators and promote a sense of vision, purpose, and passion. They do this with strong communication skills that make tasks clear, understandable, and energized.
4. Intellectual Stimulation. Leaders serve to encourage innovation from individuals, allowing risk-taking, creativity, and openness to solving problems. Individuals feel they are an integral part of the organization.

Using the Four I's in combination or alone, the school leader can begin a process of transformation for a better school organization while practicing the leadership traits and characteristics and being present in the moment for followers (Lindberg, 2022). This approach to leadership transforms teams of individuals toward their potential by having them align themselves with the vision of the work being done as communicated and facilitated by the leader. These are team efforts rather than individual efforts and provide members of the team with greater satisfaction with the work to be done (Ugochukwu, 2021).

Transformational leadership is not limited to education; other fields have also adopted this style of leadership, such as business and medicine. In medicine, for example, health care professionals are asked to deliver patient care to a higher standard, going beyond usual expectations, as they put more effort toward the patient, personal satisfaction, and pleasure in their work. By comparison, a manufacturing business might investigate a change in the concept of "quality" and "brand." This might be important to the business because of issues with past warranty problems and confusion over what the quality of the product should be. To guarantee future product quality, work needs to be done to ensure consistency over time (Lindberg, 2022).

Being a transformational leader and a respected leader go hand in hand, like good friends. This is because of the genuine, positive trust and, yes, mutual respect, that is developed to motivate and move forward the goals that will serve others (Baker & Miller, 2021). Transformational leaders inspire, guide, and motivate stakeholders to become better individuals as well as educators. Ronald Reagan (as cited by McDermott, 2024), said it very well: "The greatest leader is not necessarily the one who does the greatest things ... [the greatest leader is] the one that gets the people to do the greatest things."

One faculty member at Luis's school reflected on being hired at the school.

> Luis believed in me and gave me opportunities to grow as an educator. He absolutely believes in teachers growing professionally, moving out of their comfort zones, and taking risks. He has high expectations for his staff and is pushing us to learn and become better at our craft.

These leaders are selfless, humble, and thoughtful about others. Because of their actions, they are respected and seen as transformational. It checks the boxes of what school stakeholders need, as mentioned in an earlier chapter, such as the need to belong, be heard, and be valued.

In contrast, transactional leadership is more of a distant relative to transformational leadership. While they both influence the behavior of the stakeholders and look for performance from these individuals, this leadership approach varies greatly in how it focuses on the work to be done, the interaction with stakeholders, and how they meet vision and mission goals. Both are important leadership styles, but like some families, they tend to go their separate ways for specific reasons. Transactional leadership focuses on short-term goals, which may be predetermined, such as administering state exams on a designated date or managing a school schedule with a fixed administrative plan and due date. Transformational leadership might be interested in posing a question toward a higher purpose for the long term, such as, "What do we need to change in our curriculum and/or instruction in order for students to meet state goals and subsequently perform better on state exams?" Just to ensure there is no confusion, there are times when a transactional leadership style is necessary, required, and vital, especially when there are short-term demands. Table 8.1 compares the differences in more detail (Bass & Avolio, 1993; Milicevic, 2023).

TABLE 8.1 Transactional Leadership and Transformational Leadership

Transactional leadership	*Transformational leadership*
Manager	Influencer, visionary
Predetermined plan	Common cause
Boss	Role model
Status quo	A new way to think
Short term	Long term
Stability	Instability due to change process
Interest in the task at hand	Interest in the relationship with followers
Get the job done	Creative solutions accepted
Authoritative hierarchy	Go above and beyond
Focus on goals	Focus on stakeholder growth and goals
Targets, deadlines	Slower decision-making process due to input
Performance-based on promotions, pay (rewards, pride)	Performance-based on intrinsic satisfaction
Communication of protocol	Continuous communication and feedback

The table above points out the differences in the two styles of leadership. However, the terms should not be thought of as exact opposites, but a specific style with features based on factors such as time, mission, focus, leader motivation of self and others, sustainability, planning, work environment, and the leader's specific abilities and willingness to apply transformational leadership components to specific situations.

Detailed, practical, and realistic day-to-day examples of transformational leadership leading to substantial change in schools are difficult to find and need to be shared more. Articles tout transformational leaders like Nelson Mandela, South African president and activist; Jeff Bezos, Amazon executive; Oprah Winfrey, media mogul; Reed Hastings, Netflix founder; and this impressive list is just a humble start. And John Dewey, an educational reformer; Maria Montessori, a physician and early childhood education pioneer; and Jaime Escalante, an educator at Garfield High School in Los Angeles; are notable educational transformational leaders. The theory-to-practice transition, meaning from transformational leadership in theory to transformational leadership in practice, can be challenging; sadly, many educators think they are acting as transformational leaders but, in reality, are struggling to see any real results for their efforts. What is going wrong? To achieve at the level of the famous individuals listed here can seem impossible and unattainable. Next are some practical stories to help with that transition.

Transformational Leadership in Practice and Earning Respect

Dr. Quintin Shepherd is a published author and the former superintendent and CEO ("Chief Encouragement Officer") of Victoria Independent School District (VISD) in Victoria, Texas. Victoria is a small city in south Texas, 30 miles inland from the Gulf of Mexico. The school district enrollment in 2021–22 was 13,253 students with the following configuration of schools: one early childhood center, 14 elementary schools, four middle schools, two high schools, one Pathways in Technology Early College

High School, and two alternative schools (Victoria Independent School District, n.d.). This transformational leader went to work presenting a vision and invitation to stakeholders to participate in interactions, policies, and problems, as evidenced by statements that he shared were on the school district website such as: "Join the conversation," "Calling all community members," "Your input matters," and there was a topic called "Where are we going?" Unlike some school district vision statements that are confusing, general, wordy, and lofty, this school district vision statement is clear about who owns the educational journey. The directional statement said, "VISD remains dedicated to empowering every student, parent, and staff member with the choice to choose their unique educational journey." "Choice" was the attractive word in the statement (Victoria Independent School District, n.d.).

In an interview about Dr. Shepherd's book *The Secret of Transformational Leadership* (Dill, 2022), he talks about how school problems can fall into two categories. One category requires competent leadership because leaders see the problem as complicated and have a right or wrong outcome and a straightforward solution. The leader relies on their own knowledge, skills, and past experiences to provide solutions. An example of this would be developing a school schedule of classes for teachers and students. The second category is compassionate leadership or transformational leadership, where the solutions to a problem are unknown and the answer is complex. One person cannot serve as the "solution expert." It is better to ask for input from the stakeholders – those who will be affected by the solution – than to assume the leader knows what others need or want. This approach gives stakeholders a voice in the complex issues the school is facing.

An example of transformational leadership in practice was a call to action by Dr. Shepherd to the stakeholders in VISD as to whether the community would consider raising school taxes. A complex question, yes. It sounds like an easy, quick answer of "no," because many community members might not want to raise their taxes. Using a digital software tool called "crowdsourcing," Dr. Shepherd was able to get ideas, thoughts, and opinions from stakeholders as they responded to the question, "Should VISD seek a tax increase?" Amazingly, using this software, individuals could convene on their own time, schedule a time to share their thoughts, and find ideas with the digital tools. From there, forums were scheduled to draw upon more ideas, thoughts, suggestions, and questions from stakeholders. Besides a large number of conversations on TV and radio, other communication methods were used, input received, and plans made. Space was created for all to be heard, and at the same time, the school leader was learning from the wisdom of the group. The timetable for this was about one month and, of course, unknown hours of patience. It matters what the question (taxes) means to each person and what their perspective and opinions are. Stakeholders moved from being engaged in the problem to ownership of the solution. Even if an individual disagrees with the outcome of the question, Dr. Shepherd said, "No one can say they didn't get a chance to be heard" (Dill, 2022). Whether the stakeholder community, along with the superintendent and school board, proceeded with the tax increase or not, the foundation was laid for either decision, along with many other contributions and solutions emphasizing respect along the way. The community respected him for the process to be heard.

Stakeholders' voices point in a clear direction toward how a school leader can earn respect. It is a delicate balance to juggle all the groups' perspectives, interests, and intentions while moving forward with the school leader's vision. Where does the school leader find the time to respond to each stakeholder group? A good first step is to consider the benefits and beliefs of transformational leadership and how that fits with the school leader's personal definition of respect, school vision, mission, and leadership style. If there is a good fit, then the leader can begin to apply the elements of transformational leadership (the Four I's) to the school vision and goals when working with stakeholder groups and note the aspects that stakeholders have in common. These beginning steps of transformational leadership can be seen as the building blocks toward being a respected school leader.

"Centering" students, faculty, parents, and the community is important if we want these groups to feel welcome, equal, and heard (Lac et al., 2023). It is an interesting concept for reflection. For example, centering students could look like creating a comfortable climate for students to voice their concerns, participate in informed decision-making processes, and possibly even share a seat at the policy table facilitated by the transformational school leader. The "centering" idea could also apply to teachers, parents, and community members as these steps match their needs as well.

This space, whether digital or physical, allows groups to come together to be heard. The role of the transformational and respected school leader is to listen to individuals and introduce others to differing opinions and perspectives. It sets a higher purpose for the conversations and expectations for the participants. This yields an opportunity for the school leader to listen, grow, and earn respect from the entire school community. The following quotation simply but succinctly states how school leaders can progress forward: "Leaders earn respect when they help everyone define the paths they need to travel, are consistent in decision making, communicate well, and model in their personal and professional life the ideals the institution stands for" (Hoerr, 2009). The following are vignettes of respected school leaders in action applying a transformational leadership style.

Narratives From Respected School Leaders Involving a Transformational Leadership Style

- ♦ When trust and collaboration lead to transformation in teaching through teacher evaluation

    I convinced teachers because they trusted me after five years in the district to let me video classroom lessons. The children ignored the camera because they knew me so that I could zoom in on student work, the teacher, and the children. I immediately gave the video to the teacher to analyze, and I evaluated the video as well. Because I was respected, I would share a few quick comments with the teacher after the lesson from great things witnessed to an issue (e.g., a discipline problem if I spotted one). This was transformational because the teachers analyzed the video and they were harder on themselves looking for items that they could improve upon because they trusted me. They were professional and viewed this as professional development. They would write up their report and it became part of their file. They knew this was for improvement, for becoming a better teacher. They were very conscious that I wasn't going to use the video to be judgmental but to use it for self-improvement. If there were a staff member who needed to be evaluated because of questionable teaching, I would do a written evaluation and deliver the results. It was a really good way to get teachers to look at themselves, be introspective, and decide how they can get better. It worked. I used it for two decades. Teachers took it seriously. Tapes don't lie. I would compliment the teacher on the lesson, or if I did see something needing improvement, I would point it out. This made a difference in the lives of teachers and children and improved their instruction all because of a trustworthy, respectful relationship. The staff took becoming better to another level. One teacher told me, "I look forward to watching the video every year. My husband walked by once and said, 'Boy, you really are a great teacher!'"

- When trust, collaboration, and a shared vision transform a school program

    I wanted to create the best kindergarten program possible before full-day kindergarten programs were on the school radar. I formed a committee of teachers, parents, administrators, and even a school board member to research best practices in K programs throughout the country.

They visited several of them. Kindergarten was the first place most parents learned about our school district and that was the beginning of our reputation. As it has been said, "You never get a second chance to make a good first impression." We also used information from the National Association for the Education of Young Children for assistance. The program we developed a year later was a "gradual extended-day kindergarten program," and the schedule looked like this:

August/September 8:45–11:45 a.m.
October (stay for lunch and go home at 12:45 p.m.)
November until June (go home at 1:45 p.m.)

We had to double the number of teachers and classrooms and limit classroom enrollment based on the numbers and student needs. While it was costly, it was well worth it. Additional teachers had to be hired, and I found the most superior ones I could who understood the philosophy of our kindergarten program: no "kill and drill" workbooks. The curriculum was rewritten, and units were created that were fun and exciting, all the while teaching basic K skills and individualizing teaching and learning for all students, especially those who had special needs or for those students who could already read. This was starting fresh and, at the same time, communicating what we wanted, making the vision clear, and supporting the vision with passion and resources while taking the risk of making a large school community change.

♦ When trust, collaboration, and risk-taking transform a school and make it the hub of school community life

We started a community school with an initial grant from the central administration office so that we were able to start to provide programming for parents and students. The whole idea was to make our school a true community school. We were part of grants in the past, but this one was transformational to our school because our neighborhood was underfunded and underresourced, and this community school concept brought more parents and students to our school because of the programs we could offer. We now had cooking, culinary classes, Zumba, the arts, and musicals for students and parents, just to name a few suggested by parent and student voices. More grants came as well, such as a Disney musical grant to produce Disney junior musicals.

When I think about transformational leadership at my school, it is about the programs at the school that other schools have and we don't. If you don't have the resources, you must look for them (e.g., Home Depot for used paint for stage scenery, Jewel grocery store for packaged snacks to sell at concessions, coffee shops to learn about farm-to-table, or finding an extra pair of hands at school when needed).

Using emotional intelligence, community asset mapping, and understanding the community your school is in and its resources are key to successful partnerships and signaling where and when to reach out. Sometimes school leaders are too focused on the four walls of the school and not on the larger community. In return for their support, schools can put sponsors in newsletters with their logos (if allowable) and their unique expertise, showing and sharing their support for their school, and a respectful, collaborative partnership begins.

- ♦ When a sense of vision, purpose, and passion motivates support

    I had a vision for the school to be a performing arts school. There were no staff, supplies, or infrastructure to support this vision, so she communicated her vision to create this model, and the staff and community began to support her. As the vision for the school unfolded, she was able to hire an art teacher and a drama teacher and the process started. She changed the interior of the school with furniture to set the tone for the new school environment. People said they could feel the energy overflowing in the spaces. It was a cultural change for the school. It is now over six years since creating a school environment of love and energy and it is continuing to grow. In the past, the school was more adult-centered and not child-centered, but that has changed because of the focus of a performing arts school for children.

Children cannot see what they don't have. Just like changing the cultural aspects of the school to performing arts, we also have a new library because there wasn't one. We want children to have the best, and a school library is one of the things I wanted for them, a place for students and their families to come. I look at the library and school as the transformation of love and of themselves.

◆ When you have evidence of being a trusted, respected role model

As I walked around the school daily, I would hear my voice in the conversations of students, faculty, and/or staff saying phrases that I would say on a regular basis to emphasize the mission, vision, and core values of the school. I heard one teacher saying, "That's the Park School way to do it," meaning a student has done something special, met an academic school goal, or behaved exceptionally. "That's not the way we ever treat anyone at Park School" was also heard, referring to a student who was preparing to trip another student in the hallway, demonstrating disrespect toward a peer. These comments or sentences showed the effort it takes to have a clear, consistent, and ongoing message to the school stakeholders. Core value statements often appear as philosophical sentences or paragraphs in policy manuals, booklets, or wall posters. The statements can come to life when acted out by the leader with concrete examples. The members of the school community understood the high standards I had set being the NUMBER ONE role model and that the message had not changed over time, I believed in it and wanted to emulate and reinforce it with others. Being transformational requires the leader to walk the walk and live the talk over time.

It would be foolish to think a transformational leadership style is all rainbows and butterflies because it is not. It is respect that leads the way. A faculty member at Elena's school stated this about her leadership at the school:

> Elena is a risk-taking leader who often takes chances on her teachers. She often trusts the opinions, strategies, and skills of her faculty. When teaching at the school, I have felt safe, supported, driven, and inspired as an innovative leader. Elena somehow manages to handle everything thrown her way and overcomes challenges to better enhance the education for our students.

But not every school is lucky to have a respected school leader like Elena. It doesn't take much to derail the hard work of school change, which is an all too familiar reality in school administrative practice. If the change becomes derailed, there is a possibility that school leader respect might be next. It is smart to be aware of possible transformational sabotage that can surprise the good intentions of transformational leaders, knock them down, and have them wonder how to get up. While the following list is not all-inclusive (there are sure to be many more from your experience), hopefully it can serve as a warning label, just like the words on prescription medicine bottles or household cleaners:

TRANSFORMATIONAL LEADERSHIP WARNINGS

1. The transformational leader leaves in the middle of the work.
2. There is a leadership change at the top of the school organization.
3. There is a change of commitment to resources (e.g., time, money).
4. The vision and mission of the work seem to be altered midstream.

5. The school leader's communication to stakeholders is confusing, inconsistent, and unclear.
6. No measurements are in place to know when the goal has been reached or the end is in sight. Stakeholders are wondering, "Are we there yet?"
7. Decisions seem to be already made; however, stakeholders are still coming together in fake collegiality and collaboration. There is a history of unpleasant experiences when bringing people together or no history at all because genuinely working together was not part of the school culture.
8. Others might take credit for the work.
9. It was just a bad idea from the start.
10. There is a sense of urgency: the work must be done *now*.
11. Stakeholders are resisting.
12. When the work is completed, it lies dormant, and no one knows the next steps.
13. No recognition of the work or celebration of success is expressed publicly.
14. No one is listening or respecting diverse perspectives or opinions.
15. Plans are too grandiose and unattainable.
16. There is too much reliance on stakeholders to do the work.
17. Not everyone on the team believes in the work to be done.

♦ When a transformational leadership decision spirals downward and becomes anything but transformational

Decades ago, when some school business needs and academic technology were integrated into one technology platform, districts bought comprehensive programs like PowerSchool. I accepted the recommendation of my tech manager to hire a small company and build our own platform. We worked on it for months and months. I could see as time went on that it was not working. Later we quit and bought PowerSchool. I looked incompetent as the superintendent for doing it. I pulled the plug. I listened to my technology expert who was wrong, but I fronted it, took the heat and disappointment from the school board, and took the blame for the wasted expense. I thought we could do it. I liked the idea of individualizing and tapering the tech program to exactly our specific needs, just like individualizing/differentiating programs for all students. This vision could be listed in the expensive, failed transformational leadership attempt category except for two positive outcomes:

1. Being respected and having that reputation helped me get through this episode, primarily with my school board. It was not fun, but I knew I could get through it because I had banked enough respect currency.
2. I used it as an opportunity to publicly claim my mistake. I said, "Look at my mistake, a huge costly one." I said, "You can make mistakes too – teachers, staff, etc. There's no gain if you don't try, and sometimes you fail – look at me!" People accepted that as best they could, but I still lost a lot of "real" currency. But the message to the staff was, "Take some chances."

These examples of transformational leadership, both positive and negative, have several things in common. First, there is an honest, genuine, and brave attempt by the leader to make a substantial change. Next, leaders find evidence of progress and decide to continue or discontinue the work with proper communication. It is not unusual for transformational school leaders to make missteps (The Speaker Lab, 2024). One common misstep is balancing the need for change with the need for stability, because change, by its nature, creates uncertainty and anxiety in stakeholders. Another challenge is managing diverse teams with unique viewpoints and experiences and appreciating all voices. And let's not forget, there is going to be a dose of criticism now and again from whomever and wherever. Can the leader take it? Here is the good news! Yes! Even when projects fall apart, the transformational leader can pull the team back together by genuinely communicating and redirecting the work. By doing so, their earned respect account can increase with interest.

The promise of transformational leadership to stakeholders cannot be taken lightly (Lawrence-Lightfoot, 1999). Properly applying or blending the Four I's of transformational leadership can be challenging. The leader should call upon their strengths, traits, and behaviors, such as being a coach, mentor, listener, supporter, visionary, risk taker, or influencer, while demonstrating passion, persistence, inspiration, and creativity. And all the while, the leader is growing, learning, and increasing their superpower of respect.

Our respected school leader John, points out a transformational leadership strength that he has learned and which has been critical to his success:

> If a leader walks into a school thinking they will have immediate respect because they have a doctorate or a few years in a classroom, they will soon see the teacher brick wall [, meaning the] obstinance of teachers who are the experts and whose respect you will never get because they think and, in most instances, do have more knowledge of their classroom instruction than you ever will. Why would anyone fight that fight? It's not winnable. I think some principals see this and leave the school. My leadership characteristic is that I fight the fights I can win. I tell the teachers, "You are the experts in the classroom. I will facilitate giving you time and resources to collaborate with your peers. Through that collaboration, you will get better." All I ask of you is for me to be the main cheerleader of the school. Let me do what I do best: marketing, and you do what you do best: teach our kids. The respect comes from the staff that understand I will let them stay and be the expert in their own playground.

In summary, a transformational leadership approach must be in your repertoire of leadership styles. It can be a rewarding choice supporting your earning and maintaining respect. While transformational leadership is not a new style among leaders, it is safe to say it is a learned process. Business and medicine have shown a fondness for this leadership style as it creates strong bonds among participants, boosts job satisfaction, and produces creative solutions for these organizations, to name a few of its benefits. In education, this learned process requires a courageous leader to commit by taking an inventory of their leadership strengths, reflecting on what new knowledge, skills, competencies, attributes, and dispositions may be needed to facilitate this style, and deciding if this is the right style for the situation. Transformational leadership does bow to the situation, as no one leadership style will work in all conditions. In other words, we must ask, is this leadership style the right fit for the circumstances?

But which comes first, being a respected school leader or being a transformational school leader? It's like that old saying, "Which comes first, the chicken or the egg?" Using a transformational leadership approach helps create experiences for you to gain and maintain respect over time. In this case, being a respected leader means being a transformational leader because the leadership traits are intertwined.

Some have said transformational leadership is the holy grail of leadership (Sime, 2019). That is, transformational leadership is the ultimate achievement or success as it has lasting effects and serves both the leader and stakeholders. It also has the advantage of pushing you toward the respected school leader category.

It is brave for a leader to attempt a significant change, yet success is not guaranteed. Nonetheless, a respected school leader can use earned respect with a transformational leadership style to balance the results in their favor.

Reflection Questions:

Q1 Is there a respected transformational leader you admire?

Q2 What are you currently working on as a respected transformational leader? What have you accomplished as a respected transformational leader?

References

Baker, C., & Miller, L. H. (2021, June 16). *What is transformational leadership?* Leaders. http://www.leaders.com/articles/leadership/transformational

Bass, B. M. (1990). *Bass and Stogdill's handbook of leadership: Theory, research, and managerial applications* (3rd ed.). Free Press.

Bass, B. M., & Avolio, B. J. (1993). Transformational leadership and organizational culture. *Public Administration Quarterly*, *17*(1), 112–121.

Bass, B. M., & Avolio, B. J. (1994). *Improving organization effectiveness through transformational leadership*. Sage.

Burns, J. M. (1978). *Leadership*. Harper Collins.

Burns, J. M. (2012). *Leadership*. Open Road Media.

Clarinal, P. (2021, May 18). Influence your organizational culture through transformational leadership. *Forbes*. https://www.forbes.com/councils/forbeshumanresourcescouncil/2021/05/18/influence-your-organizational-culture-through-transformational-leadership/

Dill, K. (2022, July 11). *Dr. Quintin Shepherd – the secret to transformational leadership*. The Principal Center. https://www.principalcenter.com/dr-quintin-shepherd-the-secret-to-transformational-leadership/

Downton, J. V. (1973). *Rebel leadership: Commitment and charisma in revolutionary process*. Free Press.

Hoerr, T. (2009). The principal connection: Can leaders be popular? *Educational Leadership*, *67*(2), 92–93.

Lac, V., Mansfield, K. C., & Fernández, É. (2023). Working alongside students, parents, and families. *Phi Delta Kappan*, *105*(2), 48–52. https://doi.org/10.1177/00317217231205592

Lawrence-Lightfoot, S. (1999). *Respect: An exploration*. Perseus Books.

Lindberg, C. (2022, July 28). *Transformational leadership – explained by a CEO: Examples, pros/cons*. Leadershipahoy. https://www.leadershipahoy.com/transformational-leadership-what-is-it-pros-cons-examples/

McDermott, T. (2024, June 6). *Ronald Reagan remembered*. 60 Minutes [TV series episode]. CBS. https://www.cbsnews.com/news/ronald-reagan-remembered/

Milicevic, O. (2023, July 28). *Transformational leadership: Benefits, weaknesses, and more*. Pumble. https://pumble.com/blog/transformational-leadership/

National Association for the Education of Young Children. (n.d.). https://www.naeyc.org

Sime, C. (2019, February 5). The secret to transformational leadership. *Forbes*. https://www.forbes.com/sites/carleysime/2019/02/05/the-secret-to-transformational-leadership/

The Speaker Lab. (2024, May 7). *What is transformational leadership? Characteristics, history, and more*. https://thespeakerlab.com/blog/transformational-leadership/

Ugochukwu, C. (2021, October 4). *Transformational leadership theory*. Simply Psychology. https://www.studocu.com/bo/document/universidad-nur/auditoria/transformational-leadership-theory-simply-psychology/39553820

Van Vugt, M. (2006). Evolutionary origins of leadership and followership. *Personality and Social Psychology Review*, *10*(4), 354–371. https://doi.org/10.1207/s15327957pspr1004_5

Victoria Independent School District. (n.d.). *Home*. Retrieved November 25, 2023, from https://www.visd.net/

9

Measuring School Leader Respect

Defining School Leader Respect

The previous chapters have demonstrated the value and benefits of being respected as a school leader. Now you may ask yourself: Am I truly respected? How will I know for sure if I am respected? If respected, to what degree am I respected? This chapter will provide you with the guidance necessary to answer these questions. Let's begin.

A school leader can be defined as respected if specific administrative skills and desired personal attributes are revealed over time by the school leader to students, faculty, parents, and community stakeholders. The word *demonstrated* is used in this chapter with skills and attributes to show that they have been communicated to stakeholder groups by a leader's actions and demeanor. The degree of skills and attributes can be measured with carefully constructed, research-based stakeholder surveys. And as Peter Drucker said (as quoted in MacKenzie, 2024), "You can't manage what you can't measure."

Figure 9.1 is a Venn diagram that illustrates the integration of the demonstrated school leader respect components of effectiveness, attributes, and time. It illustrates the interconnection of a leader's demonstrated effectiveness, a leader's demonstrated attributes, and a leader's time on the job. The respected leader is the intersection of the three respect components. All three components are needed for a leader to become respected. We discuss the details of each of these components, how they work to create the respected school leader model, and how to use them to determine if you are respected.

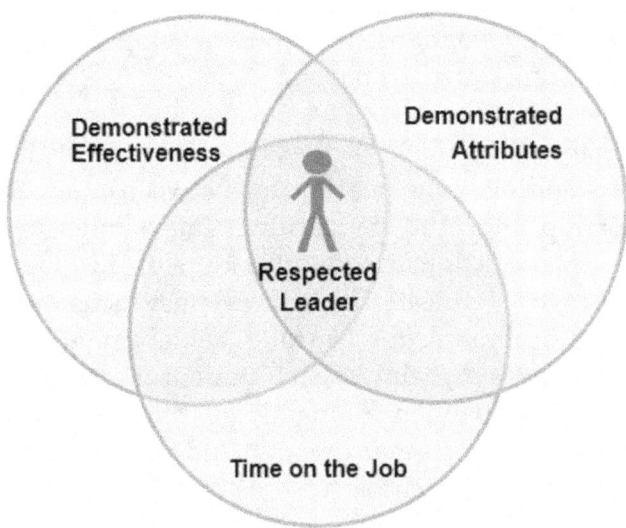

FIGURE 9.1 The Respected Leader

Demonstrated Effectiveness

For a school leader to be effective, excellent administrative skills are critical. Skills for school leaders vary depending on the position, such as school superintendent, curriculum director, principal, department chair, and so forth. While the model applies to all school leaders, the four exemplar administrators chosen for this book were sitting principals because of the large number of school principals in the United States – more than 91,000 in the 2021–22 school year, according to the Digest of Education Statistics (2023). For a school principal, these skills include recruiting and hiring excellent faculty, being knowledgeable about curriculum and instructional practices, conducting fair and impartial employee evaluations, managing the budget, and so on. A principal is effective when these leadership skills are successfully demonstrated. There are numerous leadership skills that can be found in books, state standards, leadership organizations, and local school district policy manuals. The Professional Standards for Educational Leaders (PSEL; National Policy Board for Educational Administration, 2015) enumerates specific educational leadership standards that were developed for principal effectiveness. As stated on the website:

> The Standards embody a research- and practice-based understanding of the relationship between educational leadership and student learning. Improving student learning takes a holistic view of leadership. In all realms of their work, educational leaders must focus on how they are promoting the learning, achievement, development, and well-being of each student. The Standards reflect interdependent domains, qualities, and values of leadership work that research and practice suggest are integral to student success: 1) mission, vision, and core values; 2) ethics and professional norms; 3) equity and cultural responsiveness; 4) curriculum, instruction, and assessment; 5) community of care and support for students; 6) professional capacity of school personnel; 7) professional community for teachers and staff; 8) meaningful engagement of families and community; 9) operations and management; and 10) school improvement.

The ten PSEL standards were developed over a two-year period. The website further states:

> The Council of Chief State School Officers (CCSSO) and The National Policy Board for Educational Administration (NPBEA) guided the two-year development process. It involved a thorough review of empirical research and included the input of researchers and more than 1,000 school and district leaders through surveys and focus

groups to identify gaps among the 2008 Standards, the day-to-day work of education leaders, and leadership demands of the future. After a lengthy comment and review period, CCSSO and the NPBEA boards approved the Standards.

While entirely confident in the PSEL standards being used to demonstrate the effectiveness of a school principal, one additional measure, a survey, was constructed to support whether the effectiveness of a school principal could be measured via the PSEL standards. The PSEL standards are superior and were used to construct a principal effectiveness survey instrument. To measure a school leader's demonstrated effectiveness and, ultimately, define respect for a school leader, the following survey questions were created for students in grades 6–12, faculty, parents, and the community:

A principal is effective when he/she:

1. develops, advocates, and enacts a shared mission, vision, and core values of high-quality education and academic success and well-being of each student.
2. acts ethically and professionally in personal conduct, relationships with others, decision making, stewardship of the school's resources, and all aspects of school leadership.
3. strives for equity of educational opportunity and culturally responsive practices to promote each student's success and well-being.
4. develops and supports intellectually rigorous coherent systems of curriculum, instruction, and assessment to promote each student's academic success and well-being.
5. cultivates an inclusive, caring, and supportive school community that promotes the academic success and well-being of each student.
6. develops the professional capacity and practice of school personnel to promote each student's success and well-being.

7. fosters a professional community of teachers and other professional staff to promote each student's academic success and well-being.
8. engages families and the communities in meaningful, reciprocal, and mutually beneficial ways to promote each student's academic success and well-being.
9. manages school operations and resources to promote each student's academic success and well-being.
10. acts as an agent of continuous improvement to promote each student's academic success and well-being.

Students, faculty, parents, and other community members in schools were surveyed. Their response was not about evaluating their own principal but acknowledging that the skills are needed for a school principal to be effective. The respondents were asked to place a number next to each statement using a scale of 1 (low) to 10 (high) on their agreement with the PSEL standard for a school principal to be effective. The survey results are shown in Appendix I and reflect an outstanding correlation to principal effectiveness with all PSEL standards, with stakeholder average scores ranging from 8.36 to 9.25. The authors are confident that the PSEL standards can be used in the respect surveys and for the Respected School Leader Model.

The surveys used with all four stakeholder groups to determine the leader's demonstrated skills use the language as given and have the following response options: 0 = Almost Never; 1 = Rarely; 2 = Sometimes; 3 = Usually; and 4 = Almost Always. Additional survey details can be found in the Toolkit in chapter 10.

The model discussed later in this chapter uses the principal's PSEL standards; however, the school leader should use the skills that reflect their specific position when surveying stakeholders. It is important to note skills that can be designated for school leaders can be found in state professional leader standards, job descriptions, a school leader's respective association, and articles.

Demonstrated Attributes

School administrator job applications and interview questions delve into the realm of which attributes, traits, or characteristics are required for a school leader to succeed. Words such as *honesty, empathy,* and *caring* may come to mind. Merriam-Webster defines *attribute* as "a quality, character, or characteristic ascribed to someone." A study by Goolamally and Ahmad (2014, p. 131) showed there are five important attributes that must be inherent in a school leader or principal to achieve excellence and sustainable leadership: integrity, forward-looking, inspiration, competent, and self-efficacy. The Respected School Leader Model uses specific desirable personal attributes in conjunction with administrative skills. Twelve pairs of attributes were constructed and considered critical for school leader success and, ultimately, the respect desired in a school leader. The following paired adjectives were deemed to be universally accepted as desirable attributes for success and needed for respect: accessible and approachable; caring and compassionate; collaborative and inclusive; courageous and a risk taker; courteous and polite; empathetic and sympathetic; fair and impartial; honest and trustworthy; hopeful and optimistic; humble and modest; resilient and persevering; and supportive and encouraging.

The sample group that was anonymously surveyed for effectiveness was used to validate the use of the 12 pairs of attributes in the respect survey instrument. The respondents were asked to place a number next to each statement using a scale of 1 (low) to 10 (high) on their agreement with the desired attribute in a school principal. Once again, their response was not about evaluating their principal but acknowledging that the attribute is needed in a school principal.

The survey results are shown in Appendix II and reflect outstanding correspondence to the 12 pairs of principal attributes desired, with stakeholder average scores ranging from 8.69 to 9.15. This provided confidence in using the attributes in the respect surveys and for the respected school leader model.

The surveys used with all stakeholders to determine the leader's demonstrated attributes use the language previously stated and have the following response options and numeric values: 0 = Almost Never; 1 = Rarely; 2 = Sometimes; 3 = Usually; and 4 = Almost Always. Additional survey details can be found in the Toolkit in chapter 10.

Time in School Leadership: School Size and Location

Time, like money, seems to be something many of us wish we had more of in our lives. Time is the currency that makes our ever-increasing knowledge base possible and subsequently fosters reason in how we form opinions of others. The question of time was pondered as it relates to stakeholder opinions about a school principal's effectiveness and attributes. More specifically, how long would it take a stakeholder to determine their own opinion concerning their principal's leadership skills and attributes? This would vary based on a stakeholder's interactions with their principal, how often they occur, possibly the size of the school, and perhaps even the school location (urban, suburban, or rural).

To help shed light on this, the same sample group of faculty and parents previously surveyed were asked how many months or years they needed to develop an opinion of a principal's demonstrated effectiveness and then separately a principal's demonstrated attributes. Different school sizes (small, less than 500; medium, less than 1,000, and large, over 1,000) in elementary (K–5), middle (grades 6–8), and high schools (grades 9–12) and different locations (rural, suburban, and urban) were studied. Appendices III, IV, V, and VI display the results, demonstrating that it took approximately one year to render an opinion of a school principal's effectiveness and attributes, notwithstanding size, and location.

The Respected School Leader Model: The Measure of Success

For a principal to be respected, strong administrative skills and complementary desirable personal attributes are needed. The

PSEL standards can be used to gauge a principal's effectiveness. Twelve pairs of attributes can be used to determine traits or characteristics desired and needed in a school principal. Lastly, on average, as stated previously, it takes approximately one year, with little difference when school size, or location are factored in, for faculty and parents to construct an opinion on a principal's leadership skills and attributes. The journey to respect occurs over a period of time, and the time it takes may vary due to the size of the school, and the locale of the school. Time with these groups is measured by the number of months or years of service the administrator has worked in the school. The various components work in harmony to create a picture of the leader's respect attainment or the journey toward being respected. The model has four quadrants, and the following section discusses the components of each quadrant (Figure 9.2).

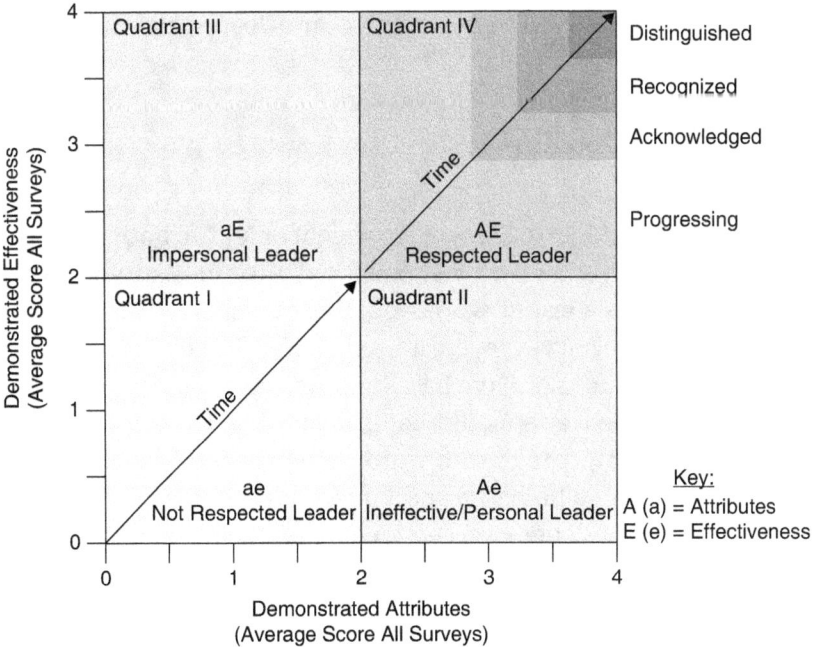

FIGURE 9.2 Demonstrated Attributes and Effectiveness

The respected school leader model includes three components. The first component is the ten PSEL standards used to determine a leader's demonstrated effectiveness. The second component is 12 descriptors or paired data points used to determine a leader's demonstrated attributes. These components are explored when surveying students in grades 6–12, faculty, parents, and community members. The third component, time, is a variable representing the leader's length of time on the job (months or years) on their journey to earn respect.

The model uses a 5-point scale (0, 1, 2, 3, 4) on the graphs to calculate survey scores. Because time varies from person to person and school to school, it is reflected in the model but not plotted specifically on the graphs. It should be taken into consideration when reviewing the results. More details of each survey used with students, faculty, parents, and other community members will be discussed later in this chapter, and they are provided in the Toolkit in chapter 10. Ultimately, the leader learns the details supporting each group's assessment of the leader's attainment of respect or the progress toward achieving respect in leader demonstrated effectiveness and leader demonstrated attributes.

The Model: Quadrant I

Quadrant I depicts low scores of 50 percent or less on both the demonstrated effectiveness and demonstrated attributes surveys. This quadrant reflects a leader who is clearly not respected at the point in time when the surveys were administered. The leader might be new on the job and not have had the time needed in the school to earn respect. The leader could have been in the job for years and is just not making progress toward being respected. The leader could also be one who had respect and then lost it. This quadrant is denoted by the letters *ae*. The lowercase *a* represents failure to achieve a score of 50 percent or more on the demonstrated attributes surveys. The lowercase *e* represents failure to achieve a score of 50 percent or more on the demonstrated effectiveness surveys. The leader in this quadrant is not respected.

The Model: Quadrant II

Quadrant II depicts medium to high scores of 50 percent or more on the demonstrated attributes surveys but low scores of less than 50 percent on the demonstrated effectiveness surveys. Quadrant II reflects a leader who is not respected at the point in time when the surveys were administered but is considered a caring, personal leader; unfortunately, though, an ineffective one. The leader is ineffective, as shown by the low effectiveness scores, but is a caring leader, as shown on the demonstrated attributes surveys. This quadrant is denoted by the letters *Ae*. The uppercase *A* represents a score of 50 percent or more on the demonstrated attributes surveys. The lowercase *e* represents failure to achieve a score of 50 percent or more on the demonstrated effectiveness surveys. The leader in this quadrant is deemed not respected because he/she has not scored 50percent or more on both demonstrated effectiveness and demonstrated attributes as required to enter the respect quadrant (Quadrant IV).

The Model: Quadrant III

Quadrant III reflects medium to high scores of 50 percent or more on the demonstrated effectiveness surveys but low scores of less than 50 percent on the demonstrated attributes surveys. This quadrant reflects a leader who is not respected at the point in time when the surveys were administered but who is effective on the job with skills but not considered a caring leader. The leader is effective with demonstrated skills but is an impersonal leader, as shown in the low scores of less than 50 percent on the attributes surveys. This quadrant is denoted by the letters *aE*. The lowercase *a* represents not having achieved a score of 50 percent or more on the demonstrated attributes surveys. The uppercase *E* represents achieving a 50 percent or more score on the demonstrated effectiveness surveys. The leader in this quadrant is not respected, as shown by the failure to score 50 percent or more on both the demonstrated effectiveness and demonstrated attributes surveys as required to enter the respect quadrant (Quadrant IV).

The Model: Quadrant IV

Quadrant IV reflects medium to high scores, 50 percent or more, on both leader demonstrated attributes and leader demonstrated effectiveness surveys. This quadrant indicates a leader who is respected. The respect quadrant has four zones with increasing levels of respect: progressing, acknowledged, recognized, and distinguished. Survey scores of 50–69 percent are labeled with the progressing level of respect. The next three respect levels are depicted by increasingly darker shades of gray: "acknowledged" with scores of 70–79 percent, "recognized" with scores of 80–89 percent, and "distinguished" with scores of 90–100 percent. This quadrant is denoted by the letters *AE*. The uppercase *A* represents a score of 50 percent or more on the demonstrated attributes surveys. The uppercase *E* represents achieving a score of 50 percent or more on the demonstrated effectiveness surveys. The leader in this quadrant is respected, having scored 50 percent or higher on both the demonstrated effectiveness and demonstrated attributes surveys.

Using the model over time will allow the leader to visualize being respected in Quadrant IV, see the progress made toward becoming respected in Quadrants II and III, or, unfortunately, see they have no respect or have regressed from being respected in Quadrant I. The journey to respect can be exciting and provide significant professional development opportunities. Sadly, the journey downward from respect can occur quickly in school administration.

The Respected School Leader Model Data Points and Implementation

The respected school leader model is designed for the leader to plot individual results of the demonstrated effectiveness and demonstrated attributes surveys from students, faculty, parents, and community members on the model. Each group is measured for individual results, and a final graph shows the averages for all four groups. Chapter 10, "The Toolkit: A Step-by-Step Guide to Measuring School Leader Respect," provides sample graphs and surveys.

The leader begins by plotting the results of the demonstrated effectiveness and demonstrated attributes survey results for each surveyed group and concludes with the average for all four groups. A scale score of 0 to 4 is used for all surveys. Each survey has the following response options and the accompanying numeric value: 0 = Almost Never; 1 = Rarely; 2 = Sometimes; 3 = Usually; and 4 = Almost Always. Students below the sixth-grade level are not surveyed and cannot be plotted in the model, but the model can be used with the other three groups. Three data points are plotted for each effectiveness and attribute instead of four.

Summary

The purpose of this chapter has been to explain the respected school leader model. The four respected school leaders discussed in this book were all determined to be respected. Using survey results and plotting demonstrated effectiveness and demonstrated attributes scores from students, faculty, parents, and other community members provides the school leader with the knowledge of whether or not respect has been attained, and, if so, what level of respect or, if not, the progress on a personalized respected school leader journey.

Note: Central office administrators, as well as school boards, local school councils, and other school governing bodies could conduct districtwide surveys with the express intent of securing individual building leader respect scores as well as an average respect score for the entire district. This could be part of their responsibility to assist the school leader with professional development opportunities.

References

Goolamally, N., & Ahmad, J. (2014). Attributes of school leaders towards achieving sustainable leadership: A factor analysis. *Journal of Education and Learning, 3*(1), 122–133.

MacKenzie, G. (2024). *If you can't measure it, you can't improve it*. Guava Box. https://guavabox.com/if-you-cant-measure-it-you-cant-improve-it/

National Center for Education Statistics. (2023). *Table 212.30: Number and percentage distribution of public and private elementary and secondary school principals, by mobility or attrition since the previous school year and occupational status: School year 2021–2022*. https://nces.ed.gov/programs/digest/d23/tables/dt23_212.30.asp

National Policy Board for Educational Administration. (2015). *Professional standards for educational leaders*. https://www.npbea.org/wp-content/uploads/2017/06/Professional-Standards-for-Educational-Leaders_2015.pdf

10

The Toolkit: A Step-by-Step Guide to Measuring School Leader Respect

This chapter aims to equip school leaders with comprehensive resources and strategic guidance to effectively implement the Respected School Leader Model. These essential tools and insights will create a pathway for school leaders to determine their level of respect and develop a collaborative professional development plan that engages and empowers the entire educational community. As John Maxwell (2013) stated, "People only follow individuals whose leadership they respect."

You will find the following sample resources in this chapter:

1. A sample email for sending the respected school leader surveys to stakeholders.
2. The effectiveness and attributes survey to be distributed to stakeholders (Table 10.1 and Table 10.2).
3. Two sample graphs plotting the level of attainment on the demonstrated effectiveness and demonstrated attributes survey (Figure 10.1 and Figure 10.2).
4. A sample graph depicting the average scores for the four stakeholder groups (Figure 10.3).

5. A sample graph showing the school leader's respect designation (Figure 10.4).

Sample Email

The sample email can be used to give participants directions for taking the survey. This email explains both parts of the survey (principal effectiveness and attributes). The two parts of the survey can be used for each group (students, faculty, parents, and community).

Dear _____,

The purpose of this anonymous survey is to obtain your beliefs and opinions regarding how well your school principal is respected. *Your responses will remain anonymous.* The survey consists of two parts: effectiveness and attributes. Your responses are most appreciated and will assist in determining the principal's respect level.

The first ten survey items ask you to respond to statements regarding your principal's effectiveness. These survey items are written exactly as they appear in the Professional Standards for Educational Leaders. Then, twelve survey items ask you to respond to your principal's attributes as demonstrated in day-to-day work. A question about how much time you need to form an opinion of your principal's effectiveness and attributes is at the end of each section. A comment section at the end of the survey allows you to share other opinions or thoughts on this topic.

Thank you in advance for your time and attention to this survey.

Sincerely,
Name and Title

Sample Survey: Effectiveness

Students/Faculty/Parents/Community

Directions: Please place a number next to each statement using the following scale:
0 = Almost Never; 1 = Rarely; 2 = Sometimes; 3 = Usually; 4 = Almost Always.

TABLE 10.1 Sample Survey: Effectiveness

PART I: EFFECTIVENESS Our school principal is effective when he/she	*(0 being lowest; 4 being highest)*
1. develops, advocates, and enacts a shared mission, vision, and core values of high-quality education and academic success and well-being of each student.	
2. acts ethically and professionally in personal conduct, relationships with others, decision making, stewardship of the school's resources, and all aspects of school leadership.	
3. strives for equity of educational opportunity and culturally responsive practices to promote each student's success and well-being.	
4. develops and supports intellectually rigorous coherent systems of curriculum, instruction, and assessment to promote each student's academic success and well-being.	
5. cultivates an inclusive, caring, and supportive school community that promotes the academic success and well-being of each student.	
6. develops the professional capacity and practice of school personnel to promote each student's success and well-being.	
7. fosters a professional community of teachers and other professional staff to promote each student's academic success and well-being.	
8. engages families and the communities in meaningful, reciprocal, and mutually beneficial ways to promote each student's academic success and well-being.	

(Continued)

TABLE 10.1 (Continued)

PART I: EFFECTIVENESS Our school principal is effective when he/she	(0 being lowest; 4 being highest)

9. manages school operations and resources to promote each student's academic success and well-being.

10. acts as agents of continuous improvement to promote each student's academic success and well-being.

Indicate how many months and/or years do you need to develop an opinion of your principal's effectiveness. _____ months _____ years

Comments:

Sample Survey: Attributes

Students/Faculty/Parents/Community

Directions: Place a number next to each statement using the following scale:
0 = Almost Never; 1 = Rarely; 2 = Sometimes; 3 = Usually; 4 = Almost Always.

TABLE 10.2 Sample Survey: Attributes

PART II – ATTRIBUTES Our school's principal is	(0 being lowest; 4 being highest)

1. accessible and approachable

2. caring and compassionate

3. collaborative and inclusive

4. courageous and a risk taker

5. courteous and polite

6. empathetic and sympathetic

7. fair and impartial

8. honest and trustworthy

(Continued)

TABLE 10.2 (Continued)

PART II – ATTRIBUTES Our school's principal is	*(0 being lowest; 4 being highest)*

9. hopeful and optimistic

10. humble and modest

11. resilient and persevering

12. supportive and encouraging

How many months or years do you need to develop an opinion of your principal's attributes?

Comments:

Sample Graphs: Demonstrated Effectiveness and Demonstrated Attributes

The respected school leader model is designed for the school leader to plot the model results of the demonstrated effectiveness and demonstrated attributes surveys from the stakeholder groups (students, faculty, parents, and community members). The example used is for only one stakeholder group, the students. The examples plotted in the student group can be replicated for faculty, parents, and community members. A scale of 0 to 4 is used for all surveys. Each survey has the following response options and the accompanying numeric value: 0 = Almost Never; 1 = Rarely; 2 = Sometimes; 3 = Usually; and 4 = Almost Always.

Demonstrated Effectiveness Example From Student Survey Responses

Figure 10.1 shows scores for student survey responses for demonstrated effectiveness. The ten PSEL standards are on the horizontal *x*-axis, and scores range from zero to four on the vertical *y*-axis. All scores for the PSEL standards are between 3.0, or "usually," and 4.0, or "almost always."

Figure 10.2 shows sample scores for student survey responses for demonstrated attributes. The 12 pairs of attributes are located on the horizontal *x*-axis, and scores range from 0 to 4 on the vertical *y*-axis. All scores for the attribute pairs are between 3.0, or "usually," and 4.0, or "almost always."

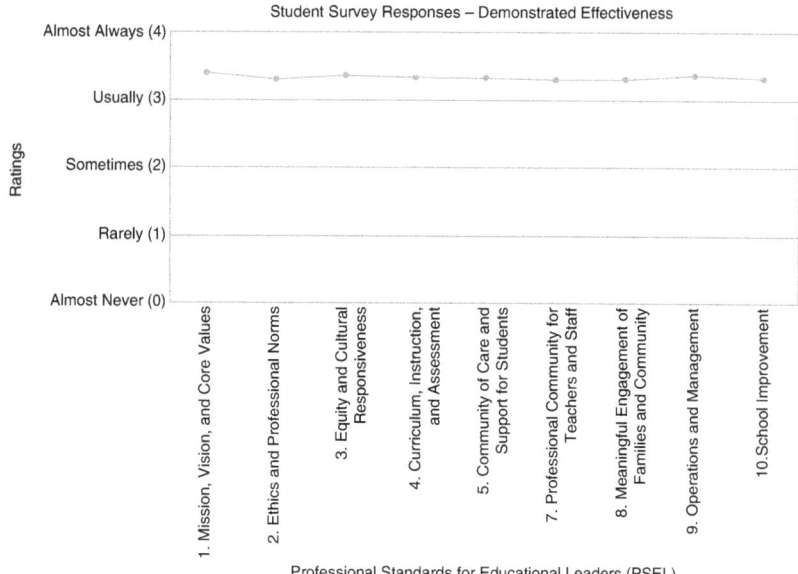

FIGURE 10.1 Demonstrated Effectiveness Example from Student Survey Responses

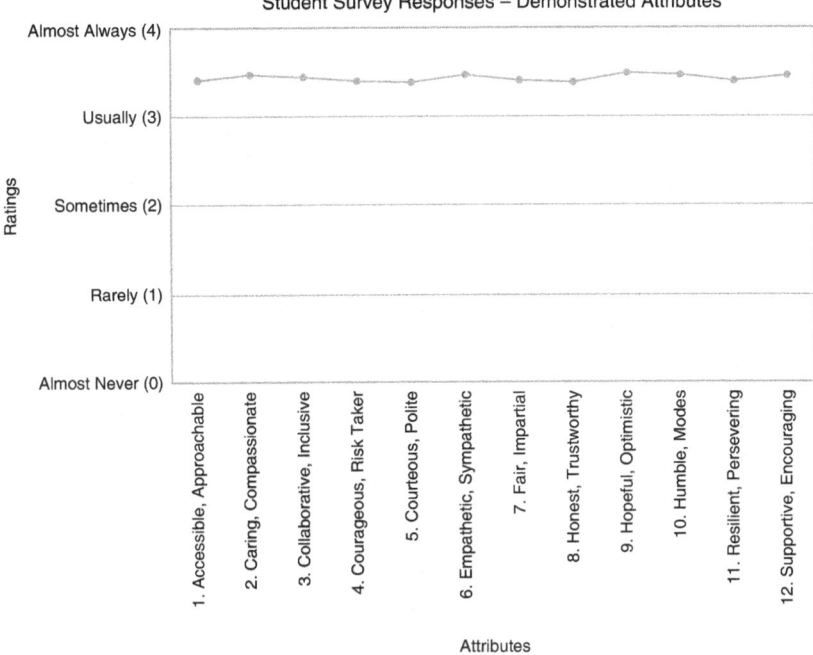

FIGURE 10.2 Demonstrated Attributes Example from Student Survey Responses

Sample Graph Depicting the Average Scores From the Four Stakeholder Groups

Figure 10.3 shows on one graph the average scores for all groups for demonstrated effectiveness and demonstrated attributes. This provides a comparison of the school leader's relative average respect scores for each group (students, faculty, parents, and other community members).

Figure 10.3 is a square divided into four equal quadrants. The horizontal x-axis indicates demonstrated attributes, the vertical y-axis demonstrated effectiveness, and each axis is numbered from 0 to 4. The quadrants are designated as follows: lower left, Quadrant I (ae); lower right, Quadrant II (Ae); upper left, Quadrant III (aE); and upper right, Quadrant IV (AE). The average scores

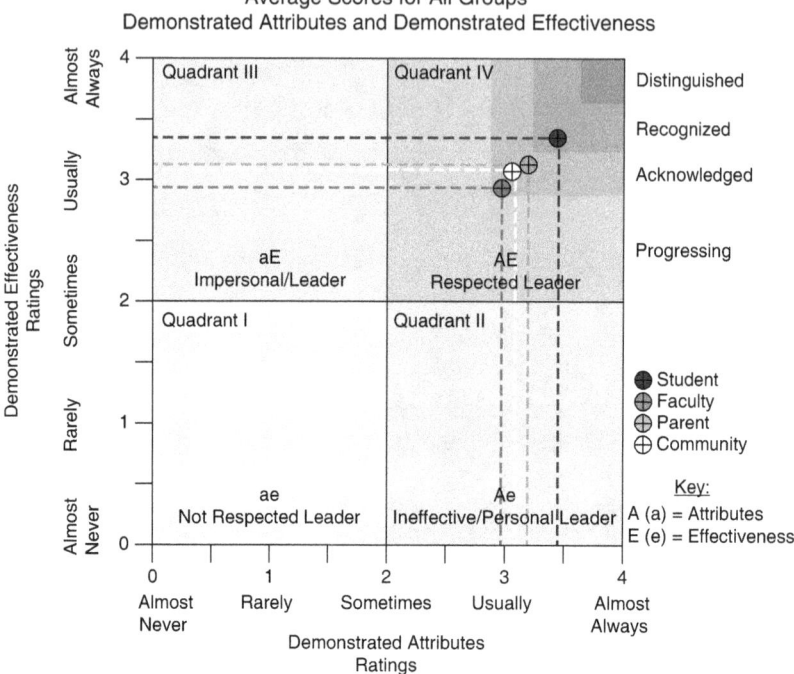

FIGURE 10.3 Average Scores for Demonstrated Attributes and Demonstrated Effectiveness for All Groups

for demonstrated attributes and demonstrated effectiveness from the students, faculty, parents, and the other community members all fall in quadrant IV.

Sample Graph Showing the School Leader's Respect Designation

Figure 10.4 provides the school leader with the overall average respect score from all four groups for demonstrated effectiveness and demonstrated attributes. Figure 10.4 places the sample school leader in the respect zone and, more specifically, in the acknowledged area. It is a square divided into four equal quadrants with the horizontal x-axis labeled demonstrated attributes, the vertical y-axis labeled demonstrated effectiveness, and each

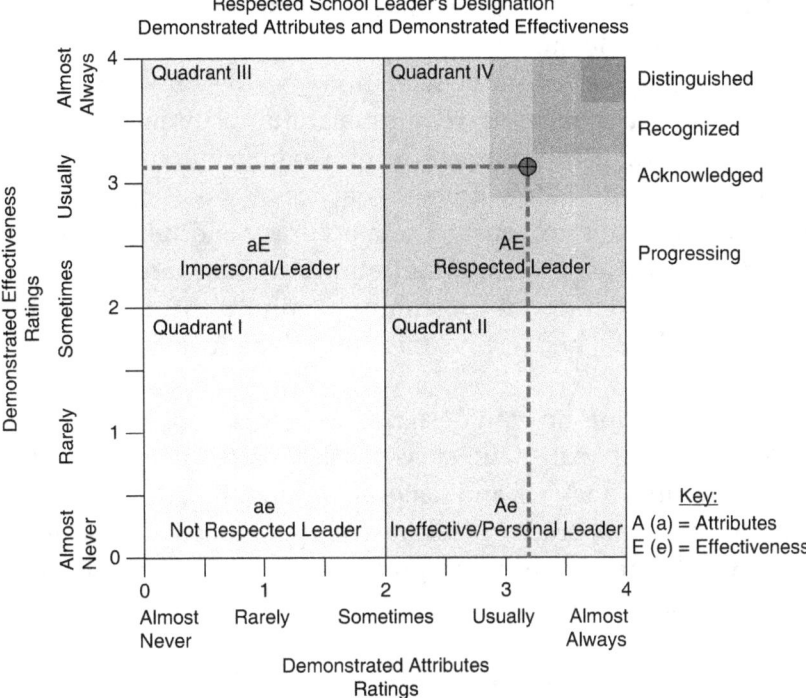

FIGURE 10.4 Respected School Leader's Designation - Demonstrated Attributes and Demonstrated Effectiveness

axis numbered from 0 to 4. The quadrants are designated as follows: lower left, Quadrant I (ae); lower right, Quadrant II (Ae); upper left, Quadrant III (aE); and upper right, Quadrant IV (AE). The average scores for demonstrated attributes and demonstrated effectiveness from the students, faculty, parents, and the other community members create one score in Quadrant IV in the "school respect acknowledged" area.

Survey Implementation: Strategies for Success

Effective survey implementation is crucial for gathering meaningful insights and driving school improvement. The following guidelines provide a comprehensive approach to designing, distributing, and leveraging surveys to maximize participation and improve data quality.

Successful survey implementation goes beyond simply creating a questionnaire. It requires careful planning, strategic execution, and a commitment to transparency and continuous improvement. By following best practices, schools can increase survey response rates, ensure data accuracy and reliability, and foster a culture of open communication and transparency. School leaders must demonstrate genuine commitment to all stakeholder feedback and create meaningful pathways for school growth.

The following tips are designed to help school leaders navigate the complexities of survey administration from initial design to final analysis and action planning. By adopting these strategies, school leaders will be well positioned to transform survey data into powerful insights that drive position change in their schools.

Tips for Successful Survey Implementation

- Ensure multilingual accessibility: Translate surveys into languages prevalent in your community to secure broader participation.
- Personalize communications: Use personalized correspondence to improve engagement and response rates.
- Utilize robust survey platforms: Employ advanced tools like Qualtrics for efficient data collection and analysis.
- Ensure impartial administration: Have a neutral third party administer the survey and collect data to maintain objectivity.
- Optimize survey timing: Avoid administering surveys during busy periods like exams or holidays, and keep them open for 2–4 weeks.
- Ensure ease of use: Provide surveys in multiple formats (online and paper-based) and ensure they are accessible to all, including those with disabilities.
- Use effective reminders: Send one or two well-timed reminders to increase response rates.

- Express gratitude: Acknowledge and thank all participants for their time and input, fostering a culture of appreciation.
- Develop and communicate action plans: Based on survey results, create detailed action plans and share them with all stakeholders to promote transparency and engagement.
- Implement follow-up surveys: Conduct periodic surveys to track progress and measure your current level of respect.

We hope this chapter will serve as a vital resource for school leaders seeking to determine and increase their respect in their communities. Providing robust tools, strategies, and insights lays the foundation for creating a transformational professional development plan. This approach enhances leadership skills and fosters a collaborative environment that engages all stakeholders in the educational community. As school leaders apply these principles and resources, they will be better equipped to navigate challenges, inspire their stakeholders, and ultimately drive positive change in their schools. The journey of a respected school leader is ongoing, and this chapter provides the essential starting point for that rewarding process.

Reference

Maxwell, J. (2013). *How successful people lead*. Center Street Hachette Book Group.

Epilogue

We began this book by sharing why you, as a school leader, should care about being respected. You carved out time in your busy schedule to read it, hoping to walk away with suggestions and ideas that will make you better at your job by being respected. You want to be the best and continue to work on this daily. So how does this book add value to your existing repertoire? If you are respected, as measured by the skills and attributes discussed, you are virtually assured of achieving student academic success in your school and much more.

Historically, a school leader's primary focus has been student academic achievement. While academic achievement is primary, many items directly affecting it have grown to include so much more to ensure that the knowledge, skills, and dispositions needed for success in life are realized. In addition to the many academic competencies required for achieving success in life, you now find yourself responsible for a litany of related items that affect academic achievement. You have to worry about and do much more for your students – even, it may seem, the impossible. You have become responsible for an ever-increasing number of items that include, but are certainly not limited to, your students' safety, social-emotional well-being, and health. The list is often added to, with few items ever removed. You are in loco parentis and play a significant role in the care and lives of your students.

Take the time to measure your skills and attributes via your school's voices and carefully reflect on the results. You will have the detailed knowledge needed and a road map of the never-ending challenges of what is expected of you as a respected school leader. The information will show that you are respected or are on your way to being respected. It will give you peace of mind and show you where to improve. There is always room for improvement, and you can be assured you are working to meet the challenges for your students and have, to a certain degree, arrived. You can take that to the bank and hopefully sleep a little bit better at night because being respected means you have succeeded.

Appendix I

Respected School Leader Instrument Validation Study: Effectiveness

A principal is effective when he/she:	Students (n=53)	Faculty (n=247)	Parents (n=127)	Community members (n=4)	Mean average (n=431)
develops, advocates, and enacts a shared mission, vision, and core values of high-quality education and academic success and well-being of each student.	8.66	9.02	9.36	8.75	9.05
acts ethically and professionally in personal conduct, relationships with others, decision making, stewardship of the school's resources, and all aspects of school leadership.	8.41	9.51	9.45	10.00	9.33
strives for equity of educational opportunity and culturally responsive practices to promote each student's success and well-being.	7.91	8.90	9.10	8.75	8.82
develops and supports intellectually rigorous, coherent systems of curriculum, instruction, and assessment to promote each student's academic success and well-being.	8.59	8.59	9.17	9.25	8.75
cultivates an inclusive, caring, and supportive school community that promotes the academic success and well-being of each student.	8.55	9.31	9.17	9.50	9.16

(Continued)

(Continued)

A principal is effective when he/she:	Students (n=53)	Faculty (n=247)	Parents (n=127)	Community members (n=4)	Mean average (n=431)
develops the professional capacity and practice of school personnel to promote each student's success and well-being.	8.27	8.91	9.39	9.00	8.96
fosters a professional community of teachers and other professional staff to promote each student's academic success and well-being.	8.24	9.15	9.35	8.00	9.10
engages families and the communities in meaningful, reciprocal, and mutually beneficial ways to promote each student's academic success and well-being.	8.24	8.76	9.20	9.75	8.84
manages school operations and resources to promote each student's academic success and well-being.	8.49	8.79	9.19	8.75	8.85
acts as an agent of continuous improvement to promote each student's academic success and well-being.	8.22	8.69	9.15	8.75	8.78
Effectiveness average	8.36	8.96	9.25	9.05	8.96

Appendix II

Respected School Leader Instrument Validation Study: Attributes

A principal should be:	Students (n=53)	Faculty (n=247)	Parents (n=127)	Community members (n=4)	Mean average (n=431)
accessible and approachable	9.19	9.58	9.38	8.50	9.46
caring and compassionate	9.18	9.28	9.20	9.75	9.25
collaborative and inclusive	8.98	9.15	9.38	8.75	9.19
courageous and a risk taker	7.42	7.95	8.13	8.00	7.93
courteous and polite	8.61	8.92	9.15	8.75	8.95
empathetic and sympathetic	8.68	9.15	9.06	8.75	9.06
fair and impartial	9.04	9.43	9.38	9.00	9.36
honest and trustworthy	9.30	9.68	9.70	10.00	9.64
hopeful and optimistic	8.38	8.72	9.10	7.00	8.73
humble and modest	8.41	8.06	8.60	9.50	8.28
resilient and persevering	8.35	9.05	9.22	8.75	9.00
supportive and encouraging	8.77	9.44	9.54	9.50	9.38
Attributes Average	8.69	9.03	9.15	8.85	9.02

Appendix III

Length of Time to Develop an Opinion of a Principal's Effectiveness by School Size

School size	Months Faculty (n=239)	Parents (n=119)	Mean average (n=358)
0–499	15.9	11.9	14.3
500–999	15.0	7.1	12.0
1000+	15.5	11.1	14.2
Overall average	15.5	10.7	13.9

Note: The mean average score is weighted because the number of respondents in the three groupings for size were not equal.

Appendix IV

Length of Time to Develop an Opinion of a Principal's Attributes by School Size

School size	Months Faculty (n=239)	Parents (n=119)	Mean average (n=358)
0–499	10.8	11.8	11.2
500–999	8.7	8.7	8.7
1000+	13.8	9.0	12.4
Overall average	12.5	9.7	11.6

Note: The mean average score is weighted because the number of respondents in the three groupings for size were not equal.

Appendix V

Length of Time to Develop an Opinion of a Principal's Effectiveness by School Location

Location	Month		
	Faculty ($n=240$)	Parents ($n=118$)	Mean average ($n=358$)
Rural	16.6	13.9	15.5
Suburban	14.2	11.2	13.2
Urban	17.4	14.3	14.7
Overall average	15.5	11.6	13.9

Note: The mean average score is weighted because the number of respondents in the three groupings for location were not equal.

Appendix VI

Length of Time to Develop an Opinion of a Principal's Attributes by School Location

Location	Month		
	Faculty $(n=240)$	*Parents* $(n=118)$	*Mean average* $(n=358)$
Rural	13.9	6.5	13.2
Suburban	11.2	11.0	11.2
Urban	14.3	8.6	11.9
Overall average	12.5	9.6	11.6

Note: The mean average score is weighted because the number of respondents in the three groupings for location were not equal.

For Product Safety Concerns and Information please contact our EU representative GPSR@taylorandfrancis.com
Taylor & Francis Verlag GmbH, Kaufingerstraße 24, 80331 München, Germany

www.ingramcontent.com/pod-product-compliance
Lightning Source LLC
Chambersburg PA
CBHW061831300426
44115CB00013B/2335